The
COAT
of
MANY
COLORS

The
COAT
of
MANY
COLORS

A devotional study of the life of Joseph

DAVID CRAIG

GOSPEL FOLIO PRESS
304 Killaly St. West, Port Colborne, ON L3K 6A6
Available in the UK from
JOHN RITCHIE LTD., Kilmarnock, Scotland

Cover design by John Nicholson III

Published by Gospel Folio Press
304 Killaly St. West
Port Colborne, ON L3K 6A6

ISBN 1-882701-83-6

Printed in the United States of America

CONTENTS

FOREWORD

Years ago in the town of Ballymena, Co. Antrim, North Ireland, where we resided for 32 years, I was privileged to share in a Gospel campaign with the late Mr. Fred Bingham. For a number of weeks the Wellington Street Hall was packed nightly. Each night during that period my message was based on an episode from the life of Joseph. These weeks proved to be a time of rich blessing.

Since then there have been great changes, and many who attended have since left the scene of time for the eternal world, entering their self-chosen destiny, never more to return. By some who are still with us, and who retain fragrant memories of the manifest presence of God that characterized the Gospel effort of those days, I have been urged to put into writing the ground that was covered, relative to my nightly messages.

During my constant going, in the Gospel and ministry until 1967, it was just impossible to find the time to engage in such a work. Since then, being greatly restricted in the work I loved so well, it meant being at home for lengthy spells, and this seemed to provide the opportunity for writing what I have entitled *The Coat of Many Colors.*

I was most happy in those days in Ballymena to share the ministry in the Gospel with our late brother Mr. Fred Bingham, whom the Lord called home to glory in August 1954. All who heard him preach appreciated his sincere and earnest appeal as he urged the audience to secure salvation through faith in Christ.

He is certainly a missed figure among the preaching fraternity in Ulster. His work is done, and now he awaits his reward from the best of Masters in the coming day of review.

As well as many Gospel lessons and appeals in the story, there are also messages for the Christian as the result of later studies. The reader will find that I have also endeavored to make much of the typical teaching from the life of Joseph as it stands in relation to the glorious person of our Lord Jesus Christ. Indeed, the end in view of this whole project is that He might be glorified, the affections of the Christian wrapped more firmly around Him, and that those who have not as yet owned Him as Saviour and Lord, will do so and become possessors of the "great salvation" so freely offered to whosoever will.

It is fitting that I should say how much I have valued the help of Mrs. Georgie Poulter who undertook the typing end of the work, and Mr. George Hall who so effectively checked the manuscript. To both of these helpers I want to express my sincere thanks.

As you read through these pages you will see that I make no claim whatever to literary genius, my only intention being to set down in writing the material gathered over the many years, praying this will prove to be the Lord's message as drawn from the life and doings of the illustrious Joseph, and that it will bring rich blessing into many a heart and home.

Yours in the Master's service,

DAVID CRAIG

THE COAT OF MANY COLORS

INTRODUCTION

The Coat of Many Colors — a rather unusual title, you say. Yes, indeed, but I would say it is not only unusual, but unique, for linked with it is one of the most fascinating and intriguing stories ever penned. Tell it to the child, and it fills him with wonder and amazement at the turn of events and the dramatic happenings of every chapter. To the advanced reader it is a classic in literature, brim full of significance as to its teaching and instruction. The believer in Christ sees it not only as a thrilling family story of ancient history, but is quick to recognize in the one who wears the "coat of many colors" many features which stand out as foreshadowings of the Lord Jesus Christ, the Saviour of the world. In First Peter 1:11, we get the prophets' search into the meaning of the "sufferings of Christ, and the glory that should follow." They were made to wonder why there must be first suffering and humiliation before exaltation and glory for the coming Messiah. It is this principle that is to govern the story of Joseph, the son of Jacob, who wore the "coat of many colors." This was to be the order of his life: first suffering, then glory; humiliation, then exaltation. The reader will see then the close link between the type and the antitype.

9

It has been said that the narrative is full of contrasts, for there we find:

LOVE AND HATRED
CORRUPTION AND CHARITY
HUMILIATION AND EXALTATION
DENIAL AND CONFESSION
RETRIBUTION AND FORGIVENESS
FAMINE AND PLENTY

No doubt this will be clearly seen as we move on, step by step, through the fascinating episodes of this thrilling narrative.

The "coat of many colors" was a distinguishing coat. The fact that Jacob gave it to Joseph made it clear that he openly recognized him as the true first-born son, with a right to the blessings associated with this honored position.

CHAPTER 1

FIRSTBORN RIGHTS

The reader may say to me, "But was not Reuben his true firstborn?" That is true. He was his firstborn by Leah; Joseph was his firstborn by Rachel. If you read First Chronicles 5:1, you will get a full answer to the reason why Joseph came into the place of the firstborn, and if you connect that Scripture passage with Genesis 49:3, 4, you will have a clear understanding why the change took place. I would ask your attention for a little to consider how, through Genesis, this principle of action is demonstrated. There is Cain and Abel; Ishmael and Isaac; Esau and Jacob; Manasseh and Ephraim — and in our story now Reuben and Joseph. In each case the second man gets priority over the first man.

Carry your thoughts now for a moment to the Lord Jesus Christ. You will notice that He is spoken of in this twofold way. He is "the firstborn" (Col. 1:15, 18; Rom. 8:29), and again in the Old Testament (Ps. 89:27); He is then called "the second man" in First Corinthians 15:47. Here is the antitype. In Genesis no firstborn could be the second man, but in the cases mentioned the second man gets the firstborn's place and blessing. Our Lord Jesus was the only One to bear the twofold title, being both the *Firstborn* and the *Second Man*. This could be developed into a most beautiful subject for a further meditation, but I leave the suggestion with my readers; it may induce you to look further into the matter.

It would be a pity to pass by the interesting story of Joseph bringing his two sons, Manasseh and Ephraim, into the presence of his aged father to receive his last blessing. He takes his firstborn son, Manasseh, and places him under the right hand of his father, and Ephraim, the second, under his left hand. But Jacob moved his hands knowingly. Indeed, he literally crossed them, so that his right hand rested on the head of Ephraim. When Joseph saw the order in which the blessing was going to be given he was displeased and protested, but old Jacob refused to change, saying to Joseph, "I know it, my son, I know it: he [Manasseh] also shall become a people, and he also shall be great: but truly his younger brother shall be greater than he, and his seed shall become a multitude of nations" (Gen. 48:19). The double blessing (that is the portion of the firstborn) is now given to Joseph; thus the "second man" is given the firstborn's place. By this the divine order is kept intact, so that the Lord Jesus Christ remains the only One who could possibly be the Firstborn and yet the Second Man at one and the same time.

It is generally accepted that the blessings of the firstborn were three in number. Earlier we drew attention to the fact that the position Joseph got should have been Reuben's. In this connection let me give you the significant paraphrase from the Jewish Targum — "To thee my son Reuben would have pertained to have received three portions above thy brethren — The Priesthood, The Kingship, The Birthright. But thou hast sinned; the Priesthood then will go to Levi, the Kingdom to Judah, the Birthright to Joseph." No doubt old Jacob was pained in making this statement. This we judge by the words that preceded the declaration, "Reuben my firstborn art thou, my strength and the beginning of my sorrow."

These then are the three blessings that went with the

firstborn in patriarchal times, but in Genesis 49 Jacob was uttering prophecy relative to the future. In Numbers 3 Levi is distinctly marked out as the priestly tribe. David's anointing in First Samuel 16:12, 13, marks Judah as the royal tribe. In Joshua 16 and 17 Joseph steps into the double portion of the inheritance through Ephraim and Manasseh. This is the birthright blessing of heirship. These Scripture passages show the fulfillment of Jacob's prophecy.

It would be interesting to have a look at the Lord Jesus Christ in these three aspects as the Firstborn. He is the Great High Priest of the Epistle to the Hebrews; at the same time He is the Royal Priest. He is Priest after the pattern of Aaron, yet also the Royal Priest out of the tribe of Judah. In a future day He will appear as King of kings (Rev. 19:16). He is called "The Lion of the tribe of Judah, the Root of David" (Rev. 5:5). In Hebrews 1:2 He is the "Heir of all things." It is plain to see that there is a beautiful link in Jacob's prophecy in Genesis 49 with our blessed Lord in relation to the threefold blessings.

CHAPTER 2

JACOB'S FIRSTBORN

We now return to Genesis 30 and consider the circumstances related to the birth of Joseph. Here Jacob begets four sons by his less-loved wife, Leah; but Rachel was barren, and this by the Lord's ordering because He saw that Leah was hated (Gen. 29:31). Such was the distress of Rachel, because no greater grief could be the portion of a Hebrew woman than to be barren. This is emphasized by her cry in verse 1, "Give me children, or else I die." At this Jacob's anger was kindled against his beloved Rachel, and he said, "Am I in God's stead, who hath withheld from thee the fruit of the womb?" At her request Jacob begets two sons by her maid, two others follow by Leah's maid, and then again two more by Leah. It would indeed be hard to gauge the depths of Rachel's misery to behold Jacob as the father of ten sons and she still a barren woman.

Then followed the dramatic change that altered the outlook of poor dejected Rachel; for we read, "And God remembered Rachel, and God hearkened to her, and opened her womb" (Gen. 30:22). Her cry had entered His ear; she had surely waited long, but now she is made to learn that "God's delays are not denials." We can almost picture her clasping her newborn babe to her breast, thrilled with the thought that it was a son, and not just a son, but the "firstborn son." Yes, she has brought into the world Jacob's divinely-given heir, he who one day would wear the coveted "coat of many colors," and eventually rise to the place of highest honor. Listen to her words: "God hath taken away my reproach," and she called his name Joseph, and said, "The Lord shall add to me another son." We can only slightly imagine the unbounded joy that filled the heart of Jacob at this act of divine intervention that removed the reproach of his beloved Rachel, and gave to him one who was to be, after Rachel, the dearest object of his affection.

The name Joseph means "adding," inferring that another son would yet be added, for she said, "The Lord will add to me another son." This was indeed a prophetic utterance fulfilled by the birth of Benjamin in Genesis 35. Can we not see a glorious truth here of our beloved Lord, the true Firstborn? What an adding was there to be as the result of the "Child born, and the Son given." In Romans 8:29 He is seen as the Firstborn among many brethren. In Hebrews, He is "bringing many sons unto glory."

Nothing more is heard of Joseph until we come to Genesis 33. In the previous chapter Jacob got the news that Esau was coming to meet him with four hundred armed men, which caused him to be "greatly afraid and distressed." Now (in chapter 33) he sees Esau approaching with his four hundred men. Look at how significantly he arranges the order of the family in readiness for any eventuality. "He put the handmaids and their children foremost, and Leah and her children after, and Rachel and Joseph hindermost" (v. 2). Oh yes, he would see to it that those whom he treasured most would be kept farthest away from danger's point. "Joseph hindermost." This strategic mode of action makes Joseph shine out as the special object of his father's love, care, and protection. Now, while it is nowhere said that Joseph was a type of Christ, the many analogies are surely most significant; these we shall see as we proceed. At this point, to begin with,

15

we can see that Joseph, a child of six years, was the special object of his father's love and affection.

> *Thus, sweet-souled Joseph, as thy life ran on,*
> *Each scene disclosed th' eternal Son,*
> *Till all thou didst, on thy meek purpose bent,*
> *Became in thee divinely eloquent,*
> *Presenting thee, in all that hurried by,*
> *The mirror of some holier history.*

—Isaac Williams

CHAPTER 3

LOVED AND HATED

Now we pass along to Genesis 37 where we find Joseph a lad of 17 years, feeding the flock with his brethren, and we read, "Joseph brought unto his father their evil report." "Now Israel loved Joseph more than all his children, because he was the son of his old age: and he made him a coat of many colors. And when his brethren saw that their father loved him more than all his brethren, they hated him, and could not speak peaceably unto him" (vv. 3, 4).

Here is one who was fondly loved, yet cruelly hated. What a picture of our Heavenly Joseph. As soon as our Lord Jesus Christ stepped out into public service, the heavens were opened, and we hear the Father say to Him, "Thou art my *beloved Son."* To the disciples on the mount the Father said, "This is my beloved Son." In John 3:35 and 5:20 the Lord Himself is heard to say, "The Father loveth the Son." Paul, in Colossians 1:13, reminds us that we have been delivered from the power of darkness, and translated into the kingdom of the Son of His Love. Yet, like Joseph, on the other hand, He was the object of cruel hatred, and that "without a cause." We hear Him say in John 7:7, "The world hateth me because I testify of it, that its works are evil."

Why He was hated is made clear in John 3:19, 20, "And this is the condemnation, that light is come into the world, and men loved darkness rather than light, because their deeds were evil. For every one that doeth evil hateth the light, neither cometh to the light, lest his deeds should be reproved." He said to His own in John 15:18, 19, "If the world hate you, ye know that it hated me before it hated you. If ye were of the world, the world would love his own: but because ye are not of the world, but I have chosen you out of the world, therefore the world hateth you." When we remember how He was treated by the leaders of the people, right throughout His earthly sojourn, and especially at its end, the cruel mockings, buffetings, spitting, scorn, the thorns, the nails, the torn back, the jibes, the torture, the shame, we get some little idea of the depth of hatred that was in the hearts of these wicked men who crucified the Lord of Glory.

Returning now to Joseph in Genesis 37, we are introduced to the garment that forms the title I selected: *The Coat of Many Colors*. This unique coat was given to Joseph by old Jacob, to mark him out as filling the distinguished position of his firstborn and rightful heir. Such treatment of the youngest brother only served to deepen the brethren's hatred and stir up the spirit of envy. What follows does not improve matters for Joseph, as we read in verse 5: "dreamed a dream, and he told it to his brethren: and they hated him yet the more." But before developing this point, let me return to the coat of many colors. Blunt, in his book *Scriptural Coincidences* sees this as a "Sacradotal Coat," something of the same idea as Aaron's, the high priest, which is called the "Garment of Glory and Beauty." Seeing that Reuben had forfeited his right to the office of priest in the family, Jacob might feel that the priesthood was open under the circumstances, and so he could by right, confer the honor upon Joseph, his firstborn by Rachel.

CHAPTER 4

THE DREAMER BECOMES A SEEKER

Having said this, we now turn to consider the first dream, which Joseph told to his brethren. "For, behold, we were binding sheaves in the field, and, lo, my sheaf arose, and also stood upright; and, behold, your sheaves stood round about, and made obeisance to my sheaf. And his brethren said to him, Shalt thou indeed reign over us? or shalt thou indeed have dominion over us? And they hated him yet the more for his dreams, and for his words" (Gen. 37:5-8).

The *Heir* now becomes the *Dreamer*. The brethren were quick to read the implication of the dream. We can imagine how they talked among themselves from their retort, "Shalt thou indeed reign and have dominion over us?" Oh, how they resented this claim to honor and dominion; to think they should stoop to do obeisance to this presumptuous lad! From deep down in their hearts rang out a united chorus of, *"Never!"*

Joseph's dreams are typical and illustrative of the predictions made by the Spirit of Christ through the Old Testament prophets of Christ's future glories (I Peter 1:11). These make Joseph in a further respect a picture of the Lord Jesus Christ, in that "He told it to his brethren." Time and again in the ministry of the blessed Lord, He spoke of the coming glory. We recall the incident when He stood before Caiaphas who said to him, "I adjure thee by the living God, that thou tell us whether thou be the Christ, the Son of God." Jesus said to him, "Thou hast said: nevertheless . . .

hereafter shall ye see the Son of man sitting on the right hand of power, and coming in the clouds of heaven." Then the high priest rent his clothes, saying, "He hath spoken blasphemy; . . . He is guilty of death" (Matt. 26:63-66). His own brethren thought Him to be beside Himself. The Pharisees, scribes, and leaders of the people, absolutely refused to accept His claim as Israel's Messiah. What folly, they said, for the carpenter of Nazareth to claim to be the Son of God, and the long-promised Messiah and deliverer of Israel. To such an impostor they would never bow. Thus He was "a man of sorrows, and acquainted with grief," despised and rejected, and hounded by them of the world as not fit to live.

Now for Joseph's second dream, which he told to his brethren, and to his father. "Behold, I have dreamed a dream more; and, behold, the sun and the moon and the eleven stars made obeisance to me. . . . and his father rebuked him, and said unto him, What is this dream that thou hast dreamed? Shall I and thy mother and thy brethren indeed come to bow down ourselves to thee to the earth?" (Gen. 37:9, 10). In his first dream it was an earthly scene; it was in the *field*. In the parable of Matthew 13 the field is the *world*. In his second dream it is a heavenly scene. We soar up into the celestial realm. This time Jacob recognizes father and mother, likewise doing homage to Joseph, and although it was true that Joseph was the chief object of his affections among his brethren, this seemed to him great presumption that the young dreamer should aspire to such greatness.

This dream, linked with the first, surely points to Him, whom "God hath highly exalted, and given a name, which is above every name: that at the name of JESUS every knee should bow, of things in heaven, and things in earth, and things under the earth; and that every tongue should confess that Jesus Christ is

Lord, to the glory of God the Father" (Phil. 2:9-11). In the case of Joseph we shall yet see his dreams literally fulfilled, but that day will only be reached by the pathway of suffering, as it truly was in the case of our glorious Lord. Just here we recall Him saying to the Emmaus travelers, "Ought not Christ to have suffered these things, and to enter into His glory? And beginning at Moses, and all the prophets, He expounded unto them in all the Scriptures the things concerning Himself."

While these dreams fed the fire of the brethren's jealousy, it is significant that 37:11 says, "But the father observed the saying," for although he could not at that time see how such a condition of things could ever obtain, yet, holding on to the promise of Abraham, and recognizing Joseph as the heir, the dreams gave him food for thought.

The attitude of the brethren here reminds us of the parable in Luke 19 where in verse 14 we have the words "We will not have this man to reign over us." What a judgment awaits these wicked enemies who despised and rejected our blessed Lord! Yes, the day of retribution will surely come. We read in verse 27 of the parable, "But those mine enemies, which would not that I should reign over them, bring hither, and slay them before me."

Can I ask you, dear reader, have you enthroned in your heart Christ as Saviour and Lord? How true are the words we sing:

> *Our Lord is now rejected,*
> *And by the world disowned,*
> *By the many still neglected,*
> *And by the few enthroned.*

I pray you, give my question your serious consideration, for those who fail to bow the knee to Him in time, will of necessity have to bow to Him in eternity, and

21

that to their eternal ruin. Allow me to quote you the words of Romans 10:9: "That if thou shalt confess with thy mouth, Jesus as Lord, and shalt believe in thine heart that God hath raised Him from the dead, thou shalt be saved" (margin).

We travel on now to the next episode where Jacob sends Joseph to Shechem to seek the welfare of his brethren and their flocks. Note the lad's willing response, "Here am I." It could be that Jacob was afraid that his sons might be in some danger, since Shechem was the district where hostility had been aroused over the matter of Dinah (Genesis 34). Joseph's ready response enables us to see him as the father's beloved son, now becoming the willing servant, going out at the father's request to seek the welfare of his brethren even though he knew that they hated him and envied him.

We follow him out of the Vale of Hebron on his way to Shechem, and if we consult a map we will see he had a long way to go. When he arrived at Shechem he learned that his brethren were not there. Here again we are caused to think of a greater than Joseph, our blessed Lord, the beloved of His Father, filling the role of the perfect Servant. It was not the Vale of Hebron He left, but the Heights of Glory. As to the length of His journey, who can measure it? We look at Bethlehem, and travel on to Calvary. What a journey! Yet it was His Father's will. We hear Him say in the Messianic Psalm 40, "Lo, I come: in the volume of the book it is written of me, I delight to do thy will, O my God." To His disciples in John 4:34, He says, "My meat is to do the will of Him that sent me, and to finish His work."

The student of Scripture delights to link up this aspect of Christ's life with the typical teaching of Leviticus 1. It is there we see a "whole burnt offering" placed on the altar for God; nothing was held back, save the skin which was the portion for the offering priest. All was placed on the altar, and as it burned it rose as a sweet-smelling savor to Jehovah. Surely this offering depicts the One whose great motive in every scene and circumstance of His life was the delight of doing the Father's will, and never more markedly than when He offered Himself without spot to God at Calvary. Here was a life wholly consumed, rising as a sweet-smelling savor, to the delight of His Father's heart. It would be well for my fellow Christian to join with me just here and ponder prayerfully Romans 12:1-2, remembering the words of Peter concerning the Lord, "He has left us an example that we should follow His steps" (1 Peter 2:21). This was surely Miss Havergal's longing and prayer, when she wrote:

> *Take my will and make it Thine,*
> *It shall be no longer mine,*
> *Take my heart; it is Thine own,*
> *It shall be Thy Royal throne.*

Thinking still of Shechem, we are told, "And a certain man found him, wandering in the field, and the man asked him saying, What seekest thou? And he said, I seek my brethren: tell me, I pray thee, where they feed their flocks? And the man said, They are departed from here, for I heard them say, Let us go to Dothan. And Joseph went after his brethren, and found them in Dothan." I am gripped with this statement, "He was found wandering in the field." Again I cannot but be reminded of Him, whom we will call the Great Seeker. J. G. Deck speaks of Him in one of his lovely hymns:

> *Wandering as a homeless Stranger*
> *In the world His hands had made.*

Mr. Deck was not thinking of Him as an aimless wanderer, but rather was thinking of the blessed Lord as a lone Stranger. Did not He Himself say to that would-

23

be disciple: "Foxes have holes, and birds of the air have nests [roosting places]; but the Son of man hath not where to lay His head" (Luke 9:58)?

> *It was a lonely path He trod,*
> *From every human soul apart;*
> *Known only to Himself and God,*
> *Was all the grief that filled His heart:*
> *Yet from the track He turned not back,*
> *Till where I lay in want and shame,*
> *He found me, blessed be His name.*

His path on earth began in a borrowed stable and ended with a borrowed cross and a borrowed tomb. As we have seen, the parable in Matthew 13 declares "the field" as the "world" (v. 38). How significant then is the type, "Joseph was found wandering in the field."

CHAPTER 5

THE DRAMA OF DOTHAN

With the information received from the man in Shechem, Joseph now makes his way to Dothan. In Genesis 37 we read, "And when they [the brethren] saw him afar off, even before he came near unto them, they conspired against him to slay him. And they said one to another, Behold, this dreamer cometh" (vv. 18, 19). The sight of "the coat of many colors" was more than they could stand, especially when they connected it with those hateful dreams. This is evident for they say, "Come now therefore, and let us slay him . . . and we shall see what will become of his dreams." Those irritating dreams! Who does he think he is? Father, mother and all of us bow down to him! The chorus of their hearts again is — "No, never!"

So deep was their hatred against the one who came seeking their welfare that they resolved to kill him there and then. But God prevented their design from taking effect. It was in the divine plan that Joseph must live. How different it was in the case of our blessed Lord: the Jews of His day were allowed to carry out their wicked designs to the full, which meant for the One who came — to seek their welfare — suffering, shame and death on Calvary's tree. Yet, blessed be God, death for Him was but the avenue to life. To John on the Isle of Patmos He said, I became dead, and behold, I am alive for evermore (Rev. 1:18).

Yes, Joseph must live, and eventually become the savior of the land, though the pathway to glory for him must also be by the way of suffering and shame. It is to be noted just here that there was one of the company who was of a different mind, and who was it but Reuben! We would say that he was the one who had most cause to envy Joseph, for the sight of "the coat of many colors" to him was a reminder of the blessing that he had forfeited, and we could understand thoughts of jealousy causing him to acquiesce in their wicked plot. Of him we read, "And Reuben heard it, and he delivered him out of their hands; and said, Let us not kill him. And Reuben said unto them, Shed no blood, but cast him into this pit that is in the wilderness, and lay no hand upon him; that he might rid him out of their hands, to deliver him to his father again" (Gen. 37:21, 22).

It is touching to notice that despite the fact of Reuben's weakness and instability which led him into grievous sin, he has the courage at this point to stand up for his brother against the united opposition. He not only desired to save Joseph's life, but also that he might be able to deliver him to his father again. However, this was not to be, just as it was in the case of Peter, who one day would have stepped in front of his loved Master to intercept Him as He was heading for Calvary with its cruel death. We hear Peter say, "Be it far from thee, Lord: this shall not be unto thee." Then comes the Lord's rebuke, "Get thee behind me, Satan: thou art an offence unto me: for thou savorest not the things that be of God, but those that be of men" (Matt. 16:22, 23). No doubt, like Reuben, Peter was moved out of pity for his loved Master, but both were out of line with the plan and purpose of God.

The next wicked and humiliating act of these callous brothers was to strip their brother of his precious "coat of many colors." What a dishonor! They would leave him without any doubt as to the fact that they had no intention of recognizing his claim as the firstborn and the father's chosen heir. Now, dishonored and disrobed, they cast him into the pit, there to languish, suffer and die, as far as they were concerned. Something that is omitted here is related later: the brethren, speaking to one another as they are held in prison, said, "We are verily guilty concerning our brother, in that we saw the anguish of his soul, when he besought us, and we would not hear . . ." (Gen. 42:21). We can only but faintly imagine the cries and wails of distress that rose up into the ears of these cruel monsters as they sat down to eat bread.

Don't you think we should pause here for a moment, and let our thoughts travel to Another who was rudely stripped of His coat? Look at the blessed Lord as seen in Matthew 27:35 — "And they crucified Him, and parted His garments, casting lots: that it might be fulfilled which was spoken by the prophet, They parted my garments among them, and upon my vesture did they cast lots." What humiliation! What shame! What dishonor! How must His sensitive and holy soul have felt to be thus treated by the creatures His hands had made, and whose good He came to seek. How callous His tormentors were, for we read, "And sitting down they watched him there."

Before proceeding I would like to comment on the kindly gesture of Reuben; even with all his faults he prevented his angry brothers from shedding innocent blood, and showed by his proposed plan, which had Joseph's rescue at heart, the true spirit of brotherhood. Of course he also knew that, being the oldest in the family, he was responsible for the care of the lad, and would be called to account by his father on their return.

Let us just here be reminded of this kindly attitude that is expected of us as brethren in our behavior one toward another. John, the apostle, put it very tersely, "We know that we have passed from death unto life, because we love the brethren. He that loveth not his brother abideth in death. Whosoever hateth his brother

27

is a murderer: and ye know that no murderer hath eternal life abiding in him" (1 John 3:14, 15). Note what follows in verse 16: "Hereby perceive we the love of God, because He laid down His life for us: and we ought to lay down our lives for the brethren." May the Lord help us to know more of this spirit and practice in our daily living, for it will make others happy; it will increase our own joy, and will bring about a closer conformity to the moral likeness of our blessed Lord.

Returning to the narrative, it seems to be that Reuben has now moved away from the pit, expecting his brethren to do the same, so that he could return in their absence and deliver Joseph. We are made to ask, Why did he not stay within sight and reach of the pit? It is plain he did not do so. Well he knew the wicked intent of the brethren, but how was he to know that they would take his absence as an opportunity to carry out their wicked design? It would seem that we have here another trait of his character, that of double-mindedness. He wanted to safeguard Joseph, yet at the same time he was away from the scene, otherwise occupied. James, in his epistle, speaks of the double-minded man as unstable in all his ways, and it is indeed remarkable, that not only does Jacob in Genesis 49:4 describe Reuben as "unstable as water," but we see also the tribe of Reuben in later days, again and again conspicuous for the same type of conduct.

There is surely a warning here for everyone, showing us that true purpose of heart must characterize our living. We cannot on the one hand have fellowship with God and on the other hand walk in worldly ways, being filled with worldly ambition. Double-minded means unsteady, fickle, staggering, reeling like a drunken man. Bunyan, in his *Pilgrim's Progress*, describes such a character as "Mr. Facing-both-ways." In contrast to this I am drawn to think of Paul's ambition in Philippians 1:20 where he says, "According to my earnest expectation and my hope, that in nothing I shall be ashamed, but that with all boldness, as always, so now also Christ shall be magnified in my body, whether it be by life, or by death." God help us to emulate this noble servant, and go on with a single purpose of heart in our lives and service for Him, so that, in the day of review we shall gain the smile of our Lord's approval.

Taking into account the sequence of events, one would be inclined to say, that everything was not going the brethren's way. They had found a way out of shedding blood, which would seem to lessen the sense of guilt, and now, as they sat down to eat bread, and to consider the next move, a company of Ishmeelite traders comes on the scene, making their way down to Egypt to market their wares. On seeing them, Judah is struck with a bright idea, and conveys it to his brethren. "What profit is it," says Judah, "if we slay our brother, and conceal his blood? Come, and let us sell him to the Ishmeelites, and let not our hand be upon him; for he is our brother and our flesh" (37: 26, 27). And his brethren were content.

Now the word "slay" is quickly dismissed from their minds and the word "sell" takes its place. They thought, This is a good plan; surely we have found the way out of the difficulty. Besides, they could see some profit to be gained out of the ingenious transaction. To have slain him would have made them no richer, but here they can get rid of the lad, and have money in their hand. Cruel monsters; you say, and indeed I agree.

See Judah as he puts forth Joseph, now stripped of "the coat of many colors," to make the sale. As the bargaining goes on, what must have been the anguish of heart felt by the terror-stricken lad, as a life of slavery stares him in the face! What tuggings at his heart-strings there must have been as he realized this

29

would be good-by to home and the Vale of Hebron, and the cause of breaking his loved father's heart! He had set out on this errand at his father's bidding. It was his brothers' welfare he came seeking. He had no hate or enmity in his heart, even though this was how they were treating him.

Thinking of Joseph in the trying circumstances in which he found himself — humiliated, dishonored and about to be sold by his own brethren for the price of a boy-slave — we immediately leap over the centuries to have our minds occupied with Another, even our own beloved Lord. We go in spirit to the Upper Room on that dread night. Among those seated at the Passover table with our Lord is the "Judah" of the New Testament. And just before going to the upper room, the Saviour utters words that most graphically describe the deep anguish of His soul, "Now is my soul troubled; and what shall I say? Father, save me from this hour; but for this cause came I unto this hour" (John 12:27). With this we link the words of Matthew 26:38, "My soul is exceeding sorrowful, even unto death." When He spoke these words He was in Gethsemane. None shall ever know the depth of agony wrung from His sinless soul effecting that heart-rending cry, "O my Father, if it be possible, let this cup pass from me . . ." (Matt. 26:39). Such was the pressure of the struggle that His sweat was, as it were, great drops of blood falling to the ground.

> *Gethsemane can I forget?*
> *Or there Thy conflict see,*
> *Thine agony and blood-like sweat,*
> *And not remember Thee?*

But we must turn now to another scene. We will watch Judas as he hurried from the upper room with the words of Jesus ringing in his ears, "What thou doest, do quickly." See him conferring with the priests and captains how he might betray his Master; and Matthew tells us, "They were glad and covenanted to give him money." Out goes the hand of Judas to receive the thirty pieces of silver, the price of a common slave.

> *Thirty pieces of silver,*
> *For the Lord of Life they gave;*
> *Thirty pieces of silver,*
> *Only the price of a slave.*

Then, from the chief priests and elders of the people, Judas is leading a great multitude, armed with swords and staves, to apprehend his Master. He knew where to find Him. He had given "them a sign, saying, Whomsoever I shall kiss, that same is He: hold Him fast. And forthwith he came to Jesus, and said, Hail, Master; and kissed Him. And Jesus said unto him, Friend, wherefore art thou come?" (Matt. 26:48-50). Luke puts it, "Judas, betrayest thou the Son of man with a kiss?" (22:48). Then they took Him and led Him away. The foul deed was done. The awful guilt now hammers at the conscience of the Satan-inspired Judas.

> *Thirty pieces of silver,*
> *Laid in Iscariot's hand;*
> *Thirty pieces of silver —*
> *And the aid of an armed band,*
> *Like a lamb that is led to the slaughter*
> *Brought the humbled Son of God,*
> *At midnight from the Garden*
> *Where His sweat had been like blood.*

Look at poor Judas as he rushes back into the presence of the chief priests and elders, bringing the money in his burning hand, saying, "I have sinned in that I have betrayed the innocent blood" (Matt. 27:4). Listen to the heartless reply of these cruel monsters, "What is that to us? See thou to that." Beside himself Judas threw the silver on the temple floor, and departed, and went and hanged himself. We can hardly imagine what must have been the remorse, the soul agony, the felt

31

terrors of an avenging God, that led him to such a state of distraction and dark despair.

> *Thirty pieces of silver,*
> *Burn on the traitor's brain;*
> *Thirty pieces of silver —*
> *Oh, it is hellish gain.*
>
> *I have sinned, and betrayed the guiltless*
> *He cried with a fevered breath,*
> *As he cast them down in the temple,*
> *And rushed to a madman's death.*

With such a meditation as this, the sobering question arises: How could it be, that one who had accompanied the blessed Lord and His beloved disciples for three and a half wonderful years, should be guilty of such a dastardly and blood-guilty act? He was even thought worthy by the other eleven to be responsible for the treasury, for he carried the bag. Although the Lord had indicated in John 6:70 and 71 that one of them would betray Him, it evidently did not sink in. Even when at the Passover, on the eve of Calvary, being troubled in spirit, the Lord said, "Verily I say unto you, that one of you shall betray me." Then the disciples looked at each other, doubting of whom He spoke, and they began to ask one after another, "Lord, is it I?" From this it is clear that the disciples did not suspect Judas.

Stop here for a moment for self-examination. How many are selling Christ today for a mere trifle! The worldling rushes blindly on in pursuit of pleasure, despite the fact that again and again an inner voice asks, "What about the claims of 'The Crucified'? What will you do with Jesus?" But, alas, the call of the alluring world drowns the inner pleadings of God's Holy Spirit. Dear reader, if this should be descriptive of the course you are pursuing, let me plead with you to stop and consider; give it a few moments' serious thought. Ask yourself, "What will the end be?" To sell Christ, and Heaven, for a vain empty world whose sinful pleasures are only "for a season," and then to know the torments of the lost throughout an unending eternity! Tell me, are you prepared to sell Christ for the eternal loss of your precious soul? Surely, never.

> *It may not be for silver,*
> *It may not be for gold,*
> *But still by tens of thousands*
> *Is the precious Saviour sold;*
> *Sold for a Godless friendship,*
> *Sold for a selfish aim,*
> *Sold for a fleeting trifle,*
> *Sold for an empty name.*
>
> *Sold in the mart of Science,*
> *Sold in the seat of power,*
> *Sold at the shrine of fortune,*
> *Sold in pleasure's bower;*
> *Sold where the awful bargain*
> *None but God's eye can see,*
> *Ponder, my soul, the question,*
> *Shall He be sold by thee?*

Before I leave this, let me ask myself and my fellow Christian, Is there not the danger that you and I could fall into this snare? One day Paul the apostle had to say regarding one who had been an associate in the work of the Gospel, "Demas hath forsaken me, having loved this present world" (2 Tim. 4:10). Let us look again at the scale of Heaven's values as presented by the Master in Luke 9:23-25: "If any man will come after me, let him deny himself, and take up his cross daily, and follow me. For whosoever will save his life shall lose it: but whosoever will lose his life for my sake, the same shall save it. For what is a man advantaged, if he gain the whole world, and lose himself, or be cast away [be disapproved]?"

While a genuine believer can never be lost, we must

never lose sight of the coming day when our lives will be reviewed by Christ. How sad to have to face it, if like a Demas, who forsook Paul, we have sold the sweetness of fellowship with and devotion to Christ for an absorbing interest in this passing scene. Take a fresh look at the cross of Christ, and say with Paul, "By which the world is crucified unto me, and I unto the world" (Gal. 6:14).

These words ring in our ears, "Judas by transgression fell" (Acts 1:25). Not "by election fell," but "by transgression fell." Let them be a warning to saved and unsaved alike as to the danger of "selling Christ" for a mere trifle, and at what a cost!

We move on in our story to see a terrorized Joseph, handed over to these heartless Ishmeelite traders, whose sole aim and object was to get him to Egypt to see what they could make on the deal. Picture in your mind poor Joseph, heartbroken, stripped of his "coat of many colors," severed from father and home, no more to see the Vale of Hebron, left only with the sombre outlook of slavery's misery in a strange land. Would he remember his dreams, and the high-rated blessing attached to the "birthright"? Surely everything must have seemed to him to be in the reverse. Yet, when we read that "the Lord was with Joseph" (Gen. 39:2), it is probable that deep in his heart there would be a settled peace such as is experienced when the Lord is consciously near.

Reuben now returns to the pit, and to his horror, finds it empty and Joseph gone. See him as he rends his clothes, and going to the brethren wails out, "The child is not; and I, whither shall I go?" No doubt, being the senior man, he knew he was responsible to see to the lad's safety, and it was he who would have to give an account to their father when they would return home. Here Reuben displays something of that instability that characterized so many of his actions, that caused the dying Jacob to speak of him as he did in Genesis 49. He had a mind to rescue Joseph, but at the same time he had a mind to go far enough away to attend to something else, so that when he did return, it was to find Joseph gone. Not only so, but his grief is soon to disappear, for he now joins the others in scheming to deceive their old father.

The "coat of many colors" comes to the fore again. We have seen that it was a "speaking coat," in that it told out the honor of the wearer, and marked him out as the loved father's heir. It spoke of the blessings of the "birthright" with no uncertain sound, and, of course, linked itself with those never-to-be-forgotten dreams, that still rankled in the minds of Joseph's brethren, and filled them with envy and hate. Now they will have to tell another lie. Watch them as they kill a little goat, take the precious coat and saturate it with the gory dye, blotting out the glory of its variegated hue. Ah, they say, this will solve the problem as to the covering of our guilt. They knew right well the conclusion the old father would come to when they would produce the coat; and, of course, it turned out just as they had planned, for when they returned they stood before the old patriarch and produced the coat saying, "This we have found: know now whether it be thy son's coat or no." And he knew it, and said, "It is my son's coat; an evil beast hath devoured him; Joseph is without doubt rent in pieces." And Jacob rent his clothes, and put on sackcloth, and mourned for his son many days. Refusing to be comforted, he said, "I will go down into the grave unto my son mourning." (See Genesis 37:32-35.)

You ask, no doubt, What kind of heart do these wicked men have, who for years were to look at their old father, burdened with grief, and brokenhearted, at the loss of his beloved son, and refusing to be comforted. Here is a faint picture of another Father and

35

Son. We never shall be able to tell what it meant to the Father of our beloved Lord who was His well-beloved and only Son, when He entered into those sufferings endured at the hands of wicked, heartless men, when He was mocked, maligned, scourged, spit upon, stripped, thorn-crowned, and nailed to the accursed tree. As we try to think of this, does it not make the words of Romans 8:32 wonderful: "He that spared not His own Son, but delivered Him up for us all"? That God should part with the darling of His bosom, knowing all that would befall Him, magnifies the greatness of His boundless love. Calvary was no afterthought of God. No doubt it was while meditating on this great theme that prompted Anne Gilbert to write these lovely words:

> What was it, O our God,
>   Led Thee to give Thy Son,
> To yield Thy well-beloved
>   For us by sin undone?
> 'Twas love unbounded led Thee thus
> To give Thy well-beloved for us.
>
> What led the Son of God,
>   To leave His throne on high,
> To shed His precious blood,
>   To suffer and to die?
> 'Twas love, unbounded love for us,
> Led Him to die and suffer thus.
>
> What moved Thee to impart
>   Thy Spirit from above,
> Therewith to fill our heart
>   With heavenly peace and love?
> 'Twas love, unbounded love to us,
> Moved Thee to give Thy Spirit thus.

CHAPTER 6

A SLAVE BOUND FOR EGYPT

Nothing is known concerning Joseph's experience as he journeyed down to Egypt with the foreign traders. At least it would be a lonely journey, and no doubt he realized as the weary hours passed that he was getting farther and farther away from father and home in Hebron's lovely vale. After Joseph was sold the first mention of him is recorded in Genesis 39:1-6:

And Joseph was brought down to Egypt; and Potiphar, an officer of Pharaoh, captain of the guard, an Egyptian, bought him of the hands of the Ishmeelites, which had brought him down thither. **And the Lord was with Joseph,** and he was a prosperous man; and he was in the house of his master the Egyptian. And his master saw that the Lord was with him, and that the Lord made all that he did to prosper in his hand. And Joseph found grace in his sight, and he served him: and he made him overseer over his house, and all that he had he put into his hand. And it came to pass from the time that he had made him overseer in his house, and over all that he had, that the Lord blessed the Egyptian's house for Joseph's sake; and the blessing of the Lord was upon all that he had in the house, and in the field. And he left all that he had in Joseph's hand; and he knew not ought he had, save the bread which he did eat. And Joseph was a goodly person, and well favoured.

Behind the wicked transaction, the hand of God was working for Joseph, leading him toward the first step of his exaltation. This turn in events shows how God "causes the wrath of man to praise Him." Little did Joseph's brethren know that the wicked and cruel treatment of their young brother was fitting into the Divine plan for the fulfillment of his dreams. No doubt they thought that getting rid of him by selling him into slavery would be the end of his dreams.

If your mind is working with mine at this point, you will be quick to call to mind Peter's word on the day of Pentecost in Acts 2:22-24: "Ye men of Israel, hear these words; Jesus of Nazareth, a man approved of God among you by miracles and wonders and signs, which God did by Him in the midst of you, as ye yourselves also know: Him, being delivered by the determinate counsel and foreknowledge of God, ye have taken, and by wicked hands have crucified and slain: Whom God hath raised up, having loosed the pains of death: because it was not possible that He should be holden of it," and in verse 36 he continues, "Therefore let all the house of Israel know assuredly, that God hath made that same Jesus, whom ye have crucified, both Lord and Christ."

Genesis 37 closes the account of Joseph being sold by his brethren into the hands of the Midianites, and they in turn selling him into Egypt. This calls to mind again in type the Lord Jesus Christ. In Pilate's judgment hall He is rejected by Israel, and delivered to the Gentiles. Although Pilate was convinced of Christ's innocence, yet to safeguard his own popularity, he hands Him over to the Roman authorities, to the cruel and ignominious death of crucifixion. From that day until the present, God has had no further dealings with Israel, not that He has cast them off forever, for as our story of Joseph ends, we see Joseph and his brethren reconciled, so it will be when God's purpose concerning the nations is complete, and "the fulness of the Gentiles be come in," Israel again shall be brought into the place of untold blessing, and Romans 11:25 and 26 describes it thus: "Blindness in part is happened to Israel, until the fulness of the Gentiles be come in. And so all Israel shall be saved: as it is written, There shall come out of Sion the Deliverer, and shall turn away ungodliness from Jacob: For this is my covenant unto them, when I shall take away their sins."

Genesis 39 introduces Joseph as the servant in the house of Potiphar. He who had worn the "son's coat," "the coat of many colors," is no longer recognized as the father's beloved son. His dress is changed, for he has now donned the "servant's coat." Surely the antitype now is seen in Philippians 2:6 and 7: "Who, being in the form of God, thought it not robbery to be equal with God: but made Himself of no reputation, and took upon Him the form of a servant, and was made in the likeness of men." In Matthew 12:18-21 God would have us fix our eye on Him when He says, "Behold My servant, whom I uphold; in whom my soul delighteth; I have put My spirit upon Him: He shall bring forth judgment to the Gentiles. . . . And in His name shall the Gentiles trust." Of course, the word "servant" is really "slave." We read of the Hebrew slave in Exodus 21:1-6. The law demanded he serve six years, then on the seventh he was to be set free. But if he desired to remain in his master's service, then "his master shall bring him unto the judges; he shall also bring him to the door, or unto the door post; and his master shall bore his ear through with an aul; and he shall serve him for ever."

It is lovely to trace our Lord through the chapters of Mark's gospel where He is portrayed in this aspect of His character. Mark omits a genealogy since a servant does not need one; what he requires is a character, and this He gets right at the outset. In chapter 1 and verses 10 and 11 our Lord is seen emerging from the waters of baptism, and as He does so, He sees the heavens opened, and the Spirit like a dove descending upon Him: "And there came a voice from heaven, saying, Thou art My beloved Son, in whom I am well pleased." Now look at the closing chapter where His work on earth is finished, to see again the heavens opened to receive the Perfect Servant, for there it is stated, "He was received up into heaven, and sat on the right hand of God." This calls to mind His own words in John 17:4, "I have glorified Thee [His Father] on the earth: I have finished the work which Thou gavest Me to do."

In Genesis 39:2 we read that "the Lord was with Joseph, and he was a prosperous man." In his service he gained the approval of his master; indeed he was held in the highest esteem, and we are told his master saw that the Lord was with him. Yes, Joseph lived daily in nearness to God, and thus he knew the value of divine enablement in making all that he did to prosper. What is more to be desired than just this? — that in one's service for the Lord, there may be a daily enjoyment of God's presence and a realization of divine help, so that in whatever environment the Lord is pleased to place us, we may there earn the smile of His approval. Joseph's approved service in the house of his foreign master would again point us to our Lord Jesus described by Peter in Acts 10:38, "How God anointed Jesus of Nazareth with the Holy Ghost and with power: who went about doing good, and healing all that were oppressed of the devil; for God was with Him."

For Joseph the place of a slave stood out in vast contrast to the privileged firstborn in the vale of Hebron wearing "the coat of many colors." But this just lets us see that circumstances matter nothing to the believer if only the Lord is with him. Moses knew the value of this when difficult and testing days lay ahead, with a "disobedient and gainsaying people," hence his cry to the Lord, "If Thy presence go not with me, carry us not up hence" (Exod. 33:15).

The fact that the Lord was with Joseph and made all that he did to prosper in his hand, drives me to Isaiah 53:10 to see that in the carrying out of the divine plan as Jehovah's Servant, there are three statements made as to our Lord's sufferings, balanced by three statements relative to His glory, the last of which is, "And the pleasure of the Lord shall prosper in His hand." How beautiful it is that in so many ways he, who wore the "coat of many colors" and then in Egypt wore "the servant's coat," typifies the Heavenly Joseph, who was the Father's true Firstborn, yet took upon Him the "form of a servant," and in that lowly guise could say, "I do always those things that please Him [the Father]" (John 8:29)!

In verse 6 of Genesis 39 it is said that "Joseph was a goodly person, and well favoured." The *Amplified Bible* says, "And now, Joseph was an attractive person and fine looking." The fact that he was now far removed from the vale of Hebron, and separated from his father's home did not change the distinctive beauty of his person or character. As to his position, truly he was now a slave, but this humiliation altered nothing relative to his unique person and standing as Jacob's firstborn son. We turn our thoughts again to our blessed Lord. While it is said in Isaiah 53:2, "He hath no form nor comeliness; and when we shall see Him, there is no beauty that we should desire Him," we have to remember this was the language of an unbelieving Israel; the veil here was covering the nation's heart. A lowly and suffering Messiah was far removed from their thoughts; they looked for a mighty, martial Monarch, who would smash to atoms the strength of the Roman Empire, and deliver them from its tyrannical rule. We are not surprised that John, at the Spirit's dictation, was made to write, "He came unto His own [things], and His own [people] received Him not" (John 1:11).

How different will be the attitude of Israel when, according to 2 Corinthians 3:16, they "turn to the Lord, the vail shall be taken away." Listen to how

41

Paul deals with this in Romans 11:25-27: "For I would not, brethren, that you should be ignorant of this mystery, lest you should be wise in your own conceits; that blindness in part is happened to Israel, until the fulness of the Gentiles be come in. And so all Israel [referring to the believing remnant] shall be saved: as it is written, There shall come out of Sion the Deliverer and shall turn away ungodliness from Jacob. For this is my covenant unto them, when I shall take away their sins."

In that coming day when He shall return in all His glory, as David's royal Son, to sit on David's royal throne, the believing remnant of Israel shall "mourn for Him, as one mourneth for his only son" (Zech. 12: 10) and acknowledge with brokenness of heart as in Isaiah 53:3-5, "He was despised and we esteemed Him not . . . But He was wounded for our transgressions, He was bruised for our iniquities: the chastisement of our peace was upon Him; and with His stripes we are healed."

While this was the nation's attitude to their Messiah, which culminated in their handing Him over to the Romans, to suffer the cruel and shameful death of crucifixion, we must not forget the many to whom the blessed Lord was The Man of attraction and beauty. Look at the wise men as they prostrate themselves before the "Ancient of Days," worshipping the Heaven-sent "King of the Jews," offering to Him "gold, frankincense, and myrrh." The gold speaks of His absolute Deity; the frankincense forecasts His life of unsullied purity; the myrrh (used for embalming a dead body) points to the Saviour's death, with its sacrificial efficacy. They saw beauty in Him. We think of those beloved and true disciples, who could not stay from Him. In John 6, when would-be disciples, not prepared to face up to the demands involved in following the "lowly Nazarene," went back, to walk no more with

Him, our blessed Lord turns to His loved disciples, that faithful little band, and says, "Will ye also go away?" Listen to Peter, the chief spokesman for the company, as he loudly protests saying, "Lord, to whom shall we go? Thou hast the words of eternal life, and we believe and are sure that Thou art that Christ, the Son of the living God" (vv. 68, 69). They saw beauty in Him.

What shall we say of those devoted women, who ministered to His needs? Just to select one, Mary of Magdala. How often we have pictured her on that Resurrection morning, wandering alone in the Garden, with a sorrowful heart, in diligent search for her loved Master. Supposing the risen Lord to be the gardener, she approaches Him, wailing out, "They have taken away my Lord, and I know not where they have laid Him . . . Sir, if thou have borne Him hence, tell me where thou hast laid Him, and I will take Him away" (John 20:13-15). Jesus said unto her, "Mary." Now she would cling to Him until He had to say, "Touch me not." Only too well she knew that no one could ever take the place of her lovely Saviour.

In concluding the witness thus borne to Him, we recall the Roman soldier who witnessed His patient suffering, and cruel agony during those dread hours on the cross. Listen to what he had to say: "Now when the centurion saw what was done, he glorified God, saying, Certainly this was a righteous man" (Luke 23:47). Please allow me to cover all these with the testimony of the spouse in Solomon's Song: "My beloved is white and ruddy, the chiefest among ten thousand . . . yea, he is altogether lovely" (5:10, 16).

As I leave this meditation, let me ask you, What does the Christ of Calvary, the Lord of Glory, mean to you? Have you ever had dealings with Him? Is He beautiful in your eyes? Have you ever bowed before His cross and thanked Him for dying for you? If not,

43

why not? Do it now! Look back to the "wondrous cross," and behold Him as the Surety dying in the sinner's place. Grasp by faith the sacrificial worth of that atoning death, and enter into the spirit of the hymn-writer's words—

He bore on the tree the sentence for me,
And now both the Surety and sinner are free.

Do this, and you will surely join the ranks of millions who say, "He is altogether lovely; this is my Beloved, and this is my Friend." A link will then have been formed with the Saviour that shall never break to the days of eternity.

CHAPTER 7

THE BLAMELESS SERVANT

Although Joseph had an upright character, and was one of whom it was said "the Lord was with him," he had to be continually on his guard. It was such a one that the cruel, subtle devil would make his target. If only he could trip him up, if he could but humiliate him, what a victory would be his! We can almost hear him chuckle with hellish glee, "We shall see what will become of his dreams." Yes, here is Joseph, a lad in his late teens, attractive and good looking, highly esteemed in the service of his master, and overseer of his house, with everything that belonged to his master under his hand and control. This brought him into daily contact with his master's wife. Little did Joseph think that hungry eyes were feasting daily on him, and that Satan had inspired her to effect his sudden downfall, precipitating him from his honored position, and hurling him into the depths of shame and disgrace.

You might ask, Why did the Lord who was with Joseph permit this? I can only answer, Wait until you have reached the end of the story, and by that time you will have found the answer. What a day this was! It was a day when his whole future was at stake. He enters as usual into the house on his daily round. Day after day she had tempted him to sin, but the God-fearing lad triumphantly stood his ground and showed her the utter folly and wickedness of such a proposal and of such a sinful act. But now, with no one in sight, she sprang and caught him by his garment, demanding her request to be then and there granted.

In such a predicament, surrounded only by what would blunt his moral sense, and render the temptation all the more powerful, what could he do? He had told her earlier, "How then can I do this great wickedness, and sin against God?" (Gen. 39:9). But what did she care? All that concerned her was to satisfy her lustful craving. What did she care, even though she ruined the honorable lad's future, and caused him to sin against his God? What could he do? Only one way of escape lay before him, and that was to flee. So at the cost of leaving his garment in her hand, he escaped the devil-laid snare, and emerged victor with a conscience void of offense. The battle was over, and the triumph won.

Let us link this with our blessed Lord's experience as He stepped out in the path of public service. Earlier we saw how Mark's gospel, the gospel of the Servant, showed that Christ was approved and highly esteemed as Jehovah's perfect Servant even as was Joseph in his master's service. From an open Heaven His commendation rang out, "Thou art my beloved Son, in whom I am well pleased." Having already said a little about this part of our Lord's character, we further notice, as with Joseph, so with the great antitype. Mark 1:12, 13 tells us: "And immediately the Spirit driveth Him into the wilderness. And He was there in the wilderness forty days, tempted of Satan; and was with the wild beasts; and the angels ministered unto Him."

It would be profitable to meditate a while and speak of this great battle fought and won by Christ, over the arch-enemy, and to see how effectually He wielded the Sword of the Spirit. Three short, pungent answers from the book of Deuteronomy, and the devil was vanquished and left to lick his sores. It is true that Satan only departed from Christ for a season, but shall I put it this way, that the defeat which he suffered that day in the wilderness was a mere pointer to that final confrontation at Calvary. Yes, that day all hell was alerted, all its might was summoned and pitted against Christ, the One of whom Paul speaks of as being "crucified through weakness" (2 Cor. 13:4).

To look at the Christ on Calvary, suffering, bleeding, dying, mocked, taunted, tortured, by God and man forsaken, we can understand in some measure Paul's words. What apparent weakness — the Maker of the universe transfixed to a Roman tree! Psalm 22:14, 15 is eloquent here, "I am poured out like water, and all my bones are out of joint: my heart is like wax; it is melted in the midst of my bowels. My strength is dried up like a potsherd; and my tongue cleaveth to my jaws; and thou hast brought me into the dust of death." Such was the heart-rending utterance of our blessed Lord during these dread hours of agony on Golgotha's tree, but there are infinitely deeper depths to be plumbed. At midday the meridian sun withheld its light — the greatest black-out the world has ever known. For three long hours it lasted, during which time the battle raged. It was then that awful cry pierced the darkness, "My God, my God, why hast Thou forsaken me?" It was then He was made "sin for us, who knew no sin; that we might be made the righteousness of God in Him" (2 Cor. 5:21).

I step aside to ask you, reader, Have you ever, by the eye of faith, seen Him there for you? For well over half a century I have sung with deepest feeling the words of Anne Ross Cousin's magnificent hymn, as she traces the deep-toned sufferings of our Lord upon the tree:

> *The tempest's awful voice was heard;*
> *O Christ, it broke on Thee!*
> *Thy open bosom was my ward;*
> *It braved the storm for me.*
> *Thy form was scarred, Thy visage marred;*
> *Now cloudless peace for me.*

47

> *Jehovah bade His sword awake;*
> *O Christ, it woke 'gainst Thee!*
> *Thy blood the flaming blade must slake,*
> *Thy heart its sheath must be;*
> *All for my sake my peace to make,*
> *Now sleeps that sword for me.*
>
> *The Holy One did hide His face;*
> *O Christ, 'twas hid from Thee!*
> *Dumb darkness wrapt Thy soul a space,*
> *The darkness due to me.*
> *But now that face of radiant grace*
> *Shines forth in light on me.*

Did the devil think, as hell shot its every shaft, and Heaven was darkened with its frown, that victory was in sight? Soon he would be disillusioned. It is true, as Hebrews 2:14 records, he "had the power of death." But listen, as the ninth hour strikes, the mighty Victor with a loud voice cries, "IT IS FINISHED": and He bowed His head, and gave up the ghost. The unseen world stands aghast. Instead of death conquering Christ, He conquers death. S. W. Gandy described this beautifully when he wrote:

> *By weakness and defeat*
> *He won the meed and crown;*
> *Trod all His foes beneath His feet*
> *By being trodden down.*
>
> *He hell in hell laid low;*
> *Made sin, He sin o'erthrew;*
> *Bowed to the grave destroyed it so,*
> *And death by dying slew.*
>
> *Bless, bless the Conqueror slain,*
> *Slain in His victory;*
> *Who lived, who died, and lives again,*
> *For thee, His church, for thee.*

I'm sure you will not blame me for staying a good while at the Cross. All this meditation, of course, sprang from the connection of the type with the great antitype. For just as Joseph was made a target for the devil, yet fought and overcame, so we have seen, it was so in greater degree with our blessed Surety. The devil had determined to do his utmost to bring Him low, but instead suffered that inglorious defeat from which he will never recover.

Returning now to Joseph's plight, we recall that he had fled from the presence of the wicked temptress. Genesis 39:14ff reads, "She called unto the men of her house, and spake unto them, saying, See, he hath brought in an Hebrew unto us to mock us; he came in unto me to lie with me, and I cried with a loud voice: And it came to pass, when he heard that I lifted up my voice and cried, that he left his garment with me, and fled, and got him out. And she laid up his garment by her, until his lord came home. And she spake unto him, according to these words . . ." Don't you feel like shouting back to her over the centuries, "You cruel, heartless, wicked woman"? His "coat of many colors" dipped in the blood of a kid was used to deceive his old father; now his "servant's coat" is used to deceive Joseph's master. It is doubtful if his master was fully convinced that his honored servant was really guilty of misconduct, even though his wife so strongly accused him. I think the sequence, as we shall see, goes to prove this.

Speaking of Joseph, it has been said that, "He would rather lose his coat, than lose his character." Before leaving this episode, let me apply the lesson. No matter who the believer is, no matter the degree of his spiritual progress (he may even be a giant in the things of God), yet no one is immune from temptation and testing. Look into the lives of the great ones of Scripture. Where is the one that has escaped, without having to undergo severe testing and battle against temptation at some time in his life? I dare not continue to pursue

49

this as the illustrations are endless. What I would say is this, that victory for Joseph in his day was gained all because his life was governed by the fear of God, and because "the Lord was with Joseph." There is no more certain safeguard in temptation's hour than a consciousness of the presence of God; this is where Joseph was living, for as we have noticed, when faced with the fierce temptation, his cry was, "How then can I do this great wickedness and sin against God?" Dear reader, let us go in for living our lives in "the fear of the Lord," so that our eyes may be kept from tears and our feet from falling.

When Potiphar listened to his wife's story, as she stood with Joseph's garment in her hand, we read, "And it came to pass, when his master heard the words of his wife, which she spake unto him . . . Joseph's master took him, and put him into the prison, a place where the king's prisoners were bound: and he was there in the prison. But the Lord was with Joseph, and showed him mercy, and gave him favor in the sight of the keeper of the prison. And the keeper of the prison committed to Joseph's hand all the prisoners that were in the prison; and whatsoever they did there, he was the doer of it" (Gen. 39:19-22).

Before leaving the matter of Joseph's temptation, it is significant to remember that Reuben, Jacob's oldest son, by primogenitor, should have had the birthright privilege, and to him should have been given "the coat of many colors," but he forfeited the right to this place of honor. How did it come about? In this way: the same temptation that Joseph faced, he faced; but alas! the unstable Reuben fell, and great was the fall. Paul, writing to Timothy, tells him to "flee youthful lusts"; he didn't say fight them, but rather to flee them. This is where Reuben failed, but this is where Joseph triumphed, and he had the victory, as I said earlier, because his life was governed by the fear of God.

Let us consider briefly Joseph's reaction. He was falsely accused. Why didn't he seek to vindicate himself? Why not tell his master the whole truth about the matter? If he had done so, and if his account was believed by Potiphar, one can imagine the awful storm that would have arisen, wrecking for all time the relationship between husband and wife. Here once more we pass to the antitype. Is not this exactly what happened in the case of our blessed Lord? I speak of Joseph's attitude in answering never a word. We travel to Pilate's judgment hall. Mark records, "And Pilate asked Him, Art Thou the King of the Jews? And He answering said unto him, Thou sayest it. And the chief priests accused Him of many things: but He answered nothing. And Pilate asked Him again, saying, Answerest Thou nothing? behold how many things they witness against Thee. But Jesus answered nothing; so that Pilate marvelled." Many witnesses were there, but they were false. Mark says, "Neither so did their witness agree together."

Just as it was with Joseph, our Lord made no attempt at self-vindication. Joseph did not utter a single word of appeal, not even a murmuring word against the cruel injustice done him as he was cast into prison. Immediately my mind flies to the prophecy of Isaiah 53:7. There it is recorded of our blessed Lord: "He was oppressed, and He was afflicted, yet He opened not His mouth: He is brought as a lamb to the slaughter, and as a sheep before her shearers is dumb, so He openeth not His mouth." With this we couple 1 Peter 2:23, "When He was reviled, reviled not again; when He suffered He threatened not; but committed His cause to Him that judgeth righteously."

Surely the lesson to learn from all this is, that when we do that which is right in the sight of God, even though we are falsely accused and the enemy may muster lying witnesses to substantiate his claim and

51

prove our guilt, the proper attitude of the believer is never to fight back, or seek recrimination. Peter puts it nicely in 1 Peter 2:20-21, "For what glory is it, if, when ye be buffeted for your faults, ye shall take it patiently? but if, when ye do well, and suffer for it, ye take it patiently, this is acceptable with God. For even hereunto were ye called: because Christ also suffered for us, leaving us an example, that ye should follow His steps." In this connection Psalm 37:5-6 is lovely: "Commit thy way unto the Lord; trust also in Him, and He shall bring it to pass. And He shall bring forth thy righteousness as the light, and thy judgment as the noonday."

Joseph had not forgotten his dreams. He knew so much of the Lord's presence with him that any suffering he had to bear, first at the hand of his cruel, heartless brethren, and now through the instrumentality of a lewd, wicked woman, could not alter the divine purpose. He had a clear sky and all was well. No doubt he could not yet see to the end of the road, but for him it was enough that "the Lord was with him."

CHAPTER 8

IN PRISON

We now consider Joseph's prison experience. The type of prison in which he was found is most suggestive. Guilty of such a crime as that of which Joseph was falsely accused, normally would have called for the death penalty, but Potiphar instead put him in "the king's prison" where he was bound with the king's prisoners. Here we are inclined to ask, Why should a God-fearing, innocent, highly respected person, as Joseph was, be asked to endure such an ordeal? Indeed, many are the examples in Scripture of the excellent of the earth, men worthy of thrones and palaces, thrown into dark and noisome dungeons. To mention but a few: Micaiah, Jeremiah, John Baptist, Peter, Paul, Silas, and since then, an army of nameless heroes who have suffered untold torture and agony, which has ended for millions in a martyr's death. Thank God, for such there is promised the "crown of life" (Rev. 2:10; James 1:12), and of which Peter says, It "fadeth not away."

Just now I have been looking at a picture which has greatly moved me. It is of a young sister in Christ in a prison camp four hundred miles from Moscow. As I now write she is there for the fourth time. Her New Testament was taken from her and she was given ten days in an isolation cell for the crime of having possessed it without the knowledge of the prison administration. Time and space forbid me to tell of others who grind in the prison camps, the record of which lies before me now. Indeed, I have introduced an endless theme, and dare not proceed further, only to ask that we bear in mind that the pathway to glory is by the avenue of suffering.

Sore trials come to the Christians from the hand of an all-wise God, yes, even to those whose lives are marked by spiritual integrity, and to such as live their lives daily in the fear of the Lord as did Joseph. Trials often are sent to test our reality, and the genuineness of our faith in the God we profess to own and trust. When silver is put into the melting pot, it affords an opportunity for removing the dross. How wonderful it is to think that severely-tried saints have known what it was, even in the white heat of suffering, to be filled with the joy of God, and loudly sing His praise!

It comes to mind now, that when that noble minister of Glasgow Cross Church was mounting the scaffold to meet a martyr's death for his allegiance to Christ, he told the by-standers, "I go up these steps today with less perturbation and fear than ever I have gone up into the pulpit to preach." Stories abound concerning these dark days of joy-filled believers hugging the very stake and praising God as the fire was roasting their very flesh.

To attempt to enumerate the many ways in which trials assail the saints of God does not come within the scope of this present work. However, just before moving on, let me submit to you one golden text from 1 Corinthians 10:13, which I call the text of the three "buts": "There hath no temptation [or trial] taken you BUT such as is common to man: BUT God is faithful, who will not suffer you to be tempted above that ye are able; BUT will with the temptation also make a way to escape, that ye may be able to bear it." He does not say that He will take you *out* of the trial, but rather, He will "make a way to escape, that you may be able to bear it."

We conclude then: that for Joseph the prison was now to be his lot, and all for the working out of the divine plan which, although yet unknown to him, was to be but the stepping stone toward the fulfillment of those wonderful dreams he had when he wore "the coat of many colors" in the vale of Hebron.

How did it fare with Joseph in prison? Note the first word of Scripture in connection with it: "But the Lord was with Joseph, and showed him mercy, and gave him favor in the sight of the keeper of the prison" (Gen. 39:21). We are made to see that the Lord, who was with him in the house as a servant, and was with him in the hour of sore and subtle temptation and gave him the victory, was still with him to support and sustain him even behind the prison bars. By and by as his integrity appeared more and more, the charge of the prisoners was committed to him, and "that which he did, the Lord made it to prosper." The whole management of the prison ultimately passed into Joseph's hands. The learned Edersheim says, "Thus, here also, Jehovah proved Himself a faithful covenant God. A silver streak was lining the dark cloud, but still patience must have her perfect work."

To answer our question more fully as to how it fared with Joseph in prison, I suggest the question demands a twofold answer. His first, and introductory term, must have been very hard to bear. Psalm 105:17-19 records something that the simple record in Genesis omits. There we read, "He sent a man before them, even Joseph, who was sold for a servant: Whose feet they hurt with fetters: he was laid in iron: Until the time that his word came: the word of the Lord tried him." Note the marginal reading of verse 18: "His soul came into iron." This would tell us that at the beginning of his imprisonment things went ill enough with Joseph, for he was made to suffer all the rigors of an eastern dungeon. Indeed, it was a most trying lot, and must have been hard to bear, despite the consciousness of innocence to sustain and console his

55

mind. In the purpose of God, all these sufferings were necessary in fitting Joseph for the upward steps that lay before him. He was to learn that even in the most trying experiences of life, God was a reality, and a very present help in trouble.

Let us learn from this: to look upon the trials and testings of life in this way; ever remembering that a loving Heavenly Father never causes his child a needless tear. Denham Smith's words in his beautiful hymn give us the experience of the trusting soul:

> *While I hear life's surging billows,*
>   *Peace, peace is mine;*
> *Why suspend my harp on willows?*
>   *Peace, peace is mine;*
> *I may sing with Christ beside me,*
> *Though a thousand ills betide me;*
> *Safely He has sworn to guide me —*
>   *Peace, peace is mine.*

> *Every trial draws Him nearer,*
>   *Peace, peace is mine;*
> *All His strokes but make Him dearer,*
>   *Peace, peace is mine;*
> *Bless I then the hand that smiteth*
> *Gently, and to heal delighteth;*
> *'Tis against my sins He fighteth —*
>   *Peace, peace is mine.*

Possibly you may not know the Lord in this intimate way. What a pity! I do indeed feel for the sinner who knows not Christ as Saviour. To whom can he turn in the storms of life, when heavy burdens oppress, when sickness and sorrow do all but break the heart? Oh, that you would come to the Saviour who waits with outstretched arms to receive you! He would fold you to His bosom, and make Himself your everlasting Friend. Then you could join in the song:

What a Friend we have in Jesus,
All our sins and griefs to bear;
What a privilege to carry
Everything to God in prayer!

To the believer the word is: "Cast thy burden upon the Lord, and He shall sustain thee" (Ps. 55:22), and again, "Casting all your care upon Him; for He careth for you" (1 Peter 5:7).

As I write, I have been trying to think about that day when Joseph arrived in prison. No doubt he would be the subject of interest among the prisoners, men with a criminal record, accustomed to finding a newcomer as one of themselves. They would be anxious to know what his crime had been, and to learn from him a lesson or two in underworld tactics. But the more they watched him the more they were filled with wonder which soon turned into admiration. Yet there is no explanation from the Hebrew youth, no trying to persuade them of the injustice of his sentence, no exposing of the guilty woman who had falsely accused him, no attempt to prove his absolute innocency. In this respect he reminds us of the Lord Jesus. I quote the words of Peter again: "When He was reviled, He reviled not again; when He suffered, He threatened not; but committed His cause to Him who judgeth righteously" (1 Peter 2:23).

From the first day the new prisoner would be closely scrutinized by the keeper of the prison. He was accustomed to receiving all kinds and classes of men, very few of whom could be trusted. Some were even dangerous and needed careful watching, while others, having learned the folly of their ways, were prepared to accept their sentence as the due reward of their deeds. "What about this strange lad of noble bearing, good-looking and attractive?" I think I hear the keeper say as he continued day by day to watch Joseph.

57

"This is no criminal; surely his cause has been mishandled and misjudged." This conviction evidently began to draw out the sympathy of his heart to this unique and mysterious character, the like of which he had never met in all his prison experience.

Not a single one of them in that house of detention knew the secret; they knew not the hidden power behind the conduct and noble bearing of the new prisoner. Verse 21 of our chapter brings all to light: "The Lord was with Joseph, and showed him mercy and gave him favor in the sight of the keeper of the prison." What a contrast there is in the garments Joseph had to wear. First it was "the coat of many colors," then the "servant's coat" in the house of Potiphar, and now it is the "criminal's coat" in the king's prison.

Joseph did not sit down and bemoan his lot, neither did he sink into a state of depression, and care not whether he lived or died. Indeed, it was just the very opposite. We find him busying himself in service to his fellow prisoners and the warders, conducting himself in such a fashion that his very influence was so much felt that, "The keeper of the prison committed to Joseph's hand all the prisoners that were in the prison." Thus he was promoted again. As C. H. Spurgeon puts it, "In the little kingdom of the prison Joseph reigned, for God was with him." It has to be remembered, too, that this was to be no mere passing event, or that his term of confinement was just a few days, until his innocence was proved. Eleven long years lay ahead before the day of release would come. While this was true, the record of Scripture tells of not a single murmur or complaint, ever escaping the lips of the innocent sufferer. He lived so near to his God day by day that he recognized that the divine ordering of his life was not his to doubt, but to be submissive, knowing that the varied experiences through which he had been called to pass, since leaving the vale of Hebron, was furthering the divine purpose, and that one day all would be made plain.

Thinking about Joseph and the way in which he bore his many and sore trials, I surely get a jolt; I am made to sit up and face this matter. I am caused to ask myself, "Do I really know anything of Joseph's patient endurance?" When I am asked to go trial's way, what is my reaction? Do I accept it in the light that such experiences all fit in with the divine plan for my life, and as a result find myself bowing in glad submission to His holy mind and will? Do I really, or do I murmur and complain and wonder, "Why me?" Others seem to sail on through life with the south wind blowing softly all the time, but with me, it's trouble, trouble all the way! Oh, to learn the lesson, dear Christian, as we thus trace the pathway of a suffering Joseph, to get near to our God, accept our trials as coming from the hand of the Father who loves us, and trust His dealings, though we may not be able to trace His designs.

Annie Johnson Flint, after years of suffering, absolutely crippled with arthritis, knew something of getting near to God in her heavy trial. Listen to her words:

He giveth more grace when the burdens grow greater,
  He giveth more strength when the labors increase,
To added affliction He addeth His mercy,
  To multiplied trials, His multiplied peace.

When we have exhausted our store of endurance,
  When strength has declined ere the day is half done,
When we reach the end of our hoarded resources,
  Our Father's full giving has only begun.

His love has no limit, His grace knows no measure,
  His power, no boundary known unto men,
For out of His infinite riches in Jesus,
  He giveth and giveth and giveth again.

Before leaving this meditation take a good look at 2 Corinthians 12:9. See Paul with a trial so hard to bear that he beseeches the Lord three times for its removal. Note the Lord's answer to his suffering servant, "My grace is sufficient for thee: for my strength is made perfect in weakness." Now note the answer of Paul, a man who lived near to his God: "Most gladly therefore will I rather glory in my infirmities, that the power of Christ may rest upon me." The Lord help us to emulate these triumphant sufferers, and may our hearts' desire find expression in the words of Sankey's hymn:

> Oh, to trust Him then more fully,
> Just to simply move
> In the conscious, calm enjoyment
> Of our Father's love,
> Knowing that life's checkered pathway
> Leadeth to His rest,
> Satisfied, the way He taketh
> Must be always best.

Little is really told us of these years of isolation, when Joseph was shut in from the outside world, but chapter 40 introduces us to one of the key incidents which goes to further the divine plan and purpose in relation to Joseph's illustrious future. How God moves in the hearts and minds of men, for the carrying out of His own designs is indeed most wonderful, as this part of our story goes to prove. At an earlier day, away back in the vale of Hebron, God used dreams, revealing the plan of God in connection with Joseph's future exaltation and glory. But to the lad who then wore "the coat of many colors," how that point was to be reached was in the realm of the unknown. There was no indication that the road to this predicted greatness would entail years of untold suffering, shame and sorrow. Rutherford's words would be eloquent to sum up these intervening years of Joseph's life:

> Deep waters crossed life's pathway,
> The hedge of thorns was sharp.

60

CHAPTER 9

THE INTERPRETER

Dreams come again into the picture in Genesis 40. This time it is two of the king's prisoners who dream, and both in the same night. I suggest you read this chapter before we proceed, for it tells the story with less words and more beauty than man ever could do.

The interest that Joseph had in the prisoners who were put to his charge comes to light in this incident. Verse 7 tells us that on the morning after the butler and baker had dreamed, Joseph looked upon them, and, behold, they were sad. Note how sympathetically he asked them, "Wherefore look ye so sad today?" Henry Law has said of this particular phrase: "Great doors swing on small hinges." And they said unto him, "We have dreamed a dream, and there is no interpreter of it." And Joseph said unto them, "Do not interpretations belong to God? Tell me them, I pray you." What prison warden would care whether his prisoners were sad or glad? His business is to see that they are kept safe and respect the rules of the prison, but this was not Joseph. His attitude toward them was one of tenderness and compassion.

In his attitude, did not Joseph resemble our blessed Lord? Surely he did. When He was here moving in and out among men and seeing the plight of fallen humanity, was not this true of Him? The prophet said of these days, "Surely He hath borne our griefs, and carried our sorrows." One day as He looked upon a starving multitude, seeing them as sheep without a shepherd, the Scripture says, "He was moved with compassion," and isn't it good to know, dear Christian, that when He went back to the glory, He went back

61

carrying with Him His real and perfect manhood, so much so that the writer of Hebrews in Chapter 4:15 tells us that, "He is touched with the feeling of our infirmities, for He was in all points tempted like as we are, yet without sin."

> *Past suffering now, the tender heart*
> *Of Jesus, on His Father's throne,*
> *Still in our sorrows shares a part,*
> *And feels them as He felt His own.*

What worried the baker and butler most was the fact that there was no interpreter. True, Joseph had had his dreams — about sheaves bowing down to his sheaf, and, sun, moon and stars doing obeisance to his star, yet he did not seem concerned that there was no interpreter for his dream. Had he had our hymn-book he might have sung in truth, "God holds the key of all unknown and I am glad." Enough it was for him that his future, though veiled, was in the hand of the Lord whom he feared, and therefore all was well. So near did Joseph live to his God that he knew, from Him, he would get the interpretation of these mysterious dreams to which he had just listened.

Joseph was careful to make it clear that interpretations belong to God. The chief butler first tells his dream, and the Lord gave Joseph its interpretation. He told the butler that within three days Pharaoh would lift up his head and restore him to his former place. Next, the baker tells his dream, but, alas, the interpretation brought heavy tidings. Joseph tells him that "within three days shall Pharaoh lift up thy head from off thee, and shall hang thee on a tree; and the birds shall eat thy flesh from off thee" (Gen. 40:19). Verses 20-22 read, "And it came to pass the third day, which was Pharaoh's birthday, that he made a feast unto all his servants . . . And he restored the chief butler unto his butlership again; and he gave the cup into Pharaoh's hand: But he hanged the chief baker: as Joseph had interpreted to them."

When Joseph told the butler that he would be restored to his place, he added, "Think on me when it shall be well with thee, and shew kindness . . . unto me, and make mention of me unto Pharaoh, and bring me out of this house: For indeed I was stolen away out of the land of the Hebrews: and here also I have done nothing that they should put me into the dungeon" (vv. 14-15). Here, for the first time, Joseph makes reference to his past, and it is beautiful to see how he relates it: "For indeed I was stolen away out of the land of the Hebrews." He did not tell how he lost his "coat of many colors," how he languished in the pit, and how for the price of a slave he was sold to the Ishmeelites. And note, though he maintained his innocence to the butler, he never told of the wicked woman who falsely accused him, and was the cause of his being in prison. Yet, withal, it would seem for the moment that a sense of frustration had gripped him and caused him to adopt a self-made plan to effect his deliverance, but, alas, his effort only led to sad disappointment, for the chapter ends with these pathetic words: "Yet did not the chief butler remember Joseph, but forgat him." At this point in Joseph's history he was caused to learn the truth of the middle verse of the Bible: "It is better to trust in the Lord than to put confidence in man" (Ps. 118:8).

For Joseph to be found in the company of the butler and the baker in prison would surely remind us of the Lord Jesus of whom it is recorded, "He was numbered with the transgressors." In each case we have two who were guilty, and one who was innocent. We travel in our thoughts to Golgotha's hill. "And there were also two other, malefactors, led with Him to be put to death. And when they were come to the place, which is called Calvary, there they crucified Him, and the

63

malefactors, one on the right hand, and the other on the left" (Luke 23:32-33). As in the case of the butler and the baker, where one was restored to life and favor, and the other was doomed to death by hanging, so we cannot help but gaze upon the three crosses — "on either side one, and Jesus in the midst."

At Calvary we see how the type fits in with the antitype. Looking first at the center cross, with its innocent Victim, we try to grapple with the great mystery. I say "mystery" because I look at the Maker of the universe, the Firstborn of all creation, the Heir of all things, the effulgence of God's glory, the exact impress of His subsistence, the Upholder of all things by the word of His power, yet, there He hangs, a spectacle of woe, crowned with thorns, battered beyond human recognition, for "His visage was so marred more than any man" (Isa. 52:14). His back had been opened with the cruel lash, and the nails hammered through those tender hands and feet. His bones were out of joint. The crowd around were mocking, jeering and taunting. His supporters had forsaken Him, but for a few devoted women and the beloved John. Stop here and have a long look at our suffering Saviour!

As Charles Wesley looked he wrote:

> 'Tis mystery all! the Immortal dies
>   Who can explore His strange design?
> In vain the first-born seraph tries
>   To sound the depths of love divine;
> 'Tis mercy all! let earth adore,
> Let angel minds inquire no more.
>
> He left His Father's throne above,
>   So free, so infinite His grace
> Emptied Himself of all but love,
>   And bled for Adam's helpless race;
> 'Tis mercy all, immense and free,
>   For, O my God, it found out me.

Mr. F. W. Boreham, the distinguished writer, says Calvary is "the center of infinities, the climax of immensities, and the conflux of eternities."

I wonder, have you ever visited Calvary to see by the eye of faith the One who "took the guilty sinner's place and suffered in his stead," and acknoweldge it was for you He died? If you never have, why not do it now? To pass Him by and refuse Him as your Saviour will mean the eternal loss of your precious soul. There is no spot so dear to the believer as Calvary. How in thought he loves to get back to Calvary! Over the years often have I sung:

> Calvary! O Calvary!
> Mercy's vast unfathomed sea,
> Love, eternal love to me:
> Saviour, we adore Thee.
>
> Darkness hung around Thy head,
> When for sin Thy blood was shed,
> Victim in the sinner's stead:
> Saviour, we adore Thee.

When preaching the Gospel I have used the following simple outline about Calvary:

1. Calvary declares Deity (John 8:28).
2. Calvary divides humanity (Luke 23:33).
3. Calvary decides destiny, and how true that is when we think of it (Luke 23:33).

We have already seen Christ in the aspect of absolute deity.

We now look at Calvary as it divides humanity. The record states, "On either side one, and Jesus in the midst." At the beginning of the awful ordeal both malefactors joined in the mockery of the sinless Sufferer; but as the torturous hours passed by, one of these by His side was moved in sympathy by the way in which Jesus was so patiently enduring the awful, inexpressible agony, and even praying for His tormentors. The other malefactor railed on Him saying, "If Thou be the Christ, save Thyself and us" (Luke 23: 39-43). But the other, answering him, rebuked him, saying, "Dost not thou fear God, seeing thou art in the same condemnation? And we indeed justly; for we receive the due reward of our deeds: but this man hath done nothing amiss." Then, turning to the Lord he said, "Lord, remember me when Thou comest into Thy kingdom." And Jesus said to him, "Verily I say unto thee, Today shalt thou be with Me in paradise."

He embraced Christ as Lord just in time, for immediately the darkness fell, and for the next three hours Christ, shut out from human gaze, must bear the full weight of Divine wrath against sin. This was the only way a righteous and sin-hating God could come out to fallen man. "The wages of sin is death." "The soul that sinneth it shall die." God, in consistency with His holy character, must punish sin, and this is just exactly what was happening during the inky darkness of Calvary. When preaching I have often quoted:

When sin first lift its deadly head,
It forced a widening span
Between the man who walked with God
And God who made the man;
With sense of sin, came sense of shame,
The naked sought to hide,
Instead of fellowship and peace,
There came the "Great Divide."

Infinite love was wounded sore,
It sought to bridge that span,
Crush out the separating wedge,
And walk again with man.
He gave His Son, His best beloved;
He came, He bled, He died,
To reconcile, He paid the price
And bridged the "Great Divide."

Yes, Calvary divides humanity. On the one side of Christ hangs a poor dying man, with his faith resting on Christ; on the other side, his companion, unrepentant, with no appreciation of Christ, dying in his sins. That is just exactly how it is in the world today. Millions have done as the dying thief did that day at Calvary. They have accepted Him as their Saviour and Surety, as the One who bore their "sins in His own body on the tree" (1 Peter 2:24). Individually they can sing:

> *He bore on the tree, the sentence for me,*
> *And now both the Surety and sinner are free.*

What a division the cross makes! That day, from the one side of Christ, the repentant thief went to be with Christ in Paradise; from the other side, the unrepentant thief in his sins went out to face retribution at the hand of a holy God, who will judge "every man according to their works" (Rev. 20:13). And so it is today, as it was then. Indeed, from the day our blessed Lord hung upon that middle cross, until the end of the day of grace, the cross ever stands as the dividing factor in the ranks of Adam's ruined race. On the one side millions rest upon its atoning sacrifice, and so are destined to share the everlasting glory of Christ, while on the other side millions pass by unheeding. I seem just now to recall the words of a great poet:

> *O highly favored Christendom,*
> *The numbers of the damned to swell,*
> *How many thousands from thee come,*
> *And louder make the wails of hell!*

In concluding this meditation on the cross we say, not only does it declare Deity, and divide humanity, but it decides destiny. The one malefactor rose to the glories of Heaven, the other dropped to the gloom of hell. I appeal to you, before passing on, whatever you

67

miss in this world, do not miss a meeting with Christ at Calvary. On this your whole eternity depends.

Forgotten by the butler, Joseph is left for two full years to grind on in prison life. Of these years we know nothing. One is left to wonder, after the disappointment of the butler's forgetfulness, would it be for him two weary years, wondering if deliverance would ever come? But he was to learn at the end of these two long years that the wheels of the Divine purpose were still turning and working, not only for his deliverance from prison, but for his advancement, and were moving toward the fulfillment of those never-to-be-forgotten dreams he had so long ago when he wore "the coat of many colors" in his father's home at Hebron's vale.

CHAPTER 10

PHARAOH'S DREAMS

Dreams again are made to fill a vital role in this intriguing drama. This time it is the great Pharaoh himself who is the dreamer. This makes us see the wonder-working ways of God, when, to further His purpose, He would disturb this mighty Potentate in the night; trouble him with dreams, which all the wise men of Egypt found impossible to unravel, or even give the slightest idea as to their meaning. Now the forgetful butler comes into prominence. You see, when he was restored to his place two years earlier, and had been asked by Joseph to sue for his deliverance, it was not God's time, nor in His plan. However, seeing Pharaoh's plight, it quickly brings to his remembrance his own dream down in the dungeon, and how the God-fearing warder solved the problem for him. Remembering his failure, relative to Joseph's request, he hastens to tell Pharaoh his experience and also that of the baker, and how true was the interpretation they received that day.

In Genesis 41:14-16 we read: "Then Pharaoh sent and called Joseph, and they brought him hastily out of the dungeon, and he shaved himself, and changed his raiment, and came in unto Pharaoh. And Pharaoh said unto Joseph, I have dreamed a dream, and there is none that can interpret it: and I have heard say of thee, that thou canst understand a dream to interpret it. And Joseph answered Pharaoh, saying, It is not in me: God shall give Pharaoh an answer of peace."

(Will you please continue to read verses 17 to 36 before you proceed farther.)

Before dealing with Pharaoh's dreams, let us note how suddenly and unexpectedly for Joseph came the end of the long, weary years of imprisonment. Did he really know that day, when obeying the call to stand before Pharaoh, as he shaved himself and changed his garments, that he was putting off "the criminal coat" never to see it again? Yet it was so. No doubt the two long years since the butler failed to remember Joseph, and his forgetting to make mention of him to Pharaoh, as had been requested, were indeed hard and lonely years, but now they are ended. God's time had arrived and the prison door must open, and "iron bars must yield."

Can we possibly forget how such a principle of dealing evidenced itself in the case of our blessed Lord? In John 2:4 we read, "Mine hour is not yet come"; in John 7:6, "My time is not yet come," and in John 8:20, "No man laid hands on Him; for His hour was not yet come." From the years of eternity His time of suffering had been measured. Yea, the very hours on dark Calvary had been arranged beforehand, in the divine plan. In John 19:28, 30 we read, "Jesus knowing that all things were now accomplished . . . said, It is finished, and He bowed His head, and gave up the ghost."

How necessary it is for us, as believers, to learn that trials cannot last longer than God's appointed time. Long ago the prophet made it known to Israel that for their waywardness, unfaithfulness and idolatry, they would have to know the rigors of Babylonish captivity for seventy years; and to Babylon they went. These were sad and sorrowful years; they hung their harps on the willows, and when asked by their captives to sing one of the Lord's songs they replied, "How can we sing the Lord's song in a strange land?" (Ps. 137:4).

The time of their captivity was to be seventy years, but not a day more, and so it was that when the time appointed had arrived, God put it into the heart of Cyrus, a heathen monarch, to make a decree allowing them to return to their own land.

Oh, that we might learn, as did Joseph and the captives in Babylon, that deliverance from trial is timed by a loving Heavenly Father "Who will not suffer you to be tempted [tried] above that you are able" (1 Cor. 10:13). He will pass through the waters with us, and will not allow them to overflow us. Yes, we have "a Father that will never cause His child a needless tear."

Joseph has another change of coat. We call it "The Seer's Coat," for this is how he is presented to Pharaoh. As Joseph told the butler two years before that interpretations belong to God, so now he tells Pharaoh, "God shall give Pharaoh an answer of peace." When Joseph was about to unravel the meaning of such a baffling dream, he said to the monarch, "God hath showed Pharaoh what He is about to do." He made it clear that he was but the mouthpiece of the God whom he feared and served. Occasions like this let us into the secret of Joseph's humility and dependence upon his God, and in this we have a faint type of the blessed Lord while He was here among men. We hear Him say in John 12:48, "He that rejecteth Me, and receiveth not My words, hath one that judgeth him: the word that I have spoken, the same shall judge him in the last day. For I have not spoken of myself; but the Father which sent Me, He gave Me a commandment, what I should say, and what I should speak. And I know that His commandment is life everlasting: whatsoever I speak therefore, even as the Father said unto Me, so I speak." Such words surely point Him out as "the dependent Man" and as "Jehovah's perfect Servant."

The interpretation God gave to Joseph was really

71

a prophecy, for it foretold the character of the fourteen years that lay ahead. The seven lean cattle which Pharaoh saw in his dream, devouring the seven fat cattle, and yet no fatter as the result; and the one stalk of corn with seven ears "full and good" having another stalk springing up beside it, "but blasted with the east wind," and these thin ears devouring the seven good ears, were, according to the interpretation, seven years of great plenty in Egypt, to be followed by seven years of grievous famine, the impact of which would be felt worldwide. This eventful period was to commence immediately, for Joseph told Pharaoh in verse 32 the reason for the dream being repeated was that the thing was established by God, and God would shortly bring it to pass, and his advice to Pharaoh is found in verses 33 to 43.

CHAPTER 11

HUMILIATION — EXALTATION

Now therefore let Pharaoh look out a man discreet and wise, and set him over the land of Egypt. Let Pharaoh do this, and let him appoint officers over the land, and take up the fifth part of the land of Egypt in the seven plenteous years. And let them gather all the food of those good years that come, and lay up corn under the hand of Pharaoh, and let them keep food in the cities. And that food shall be for store to the land against the seven years of famine, which shall be in the land of Egypt; that the land perish not through the famine. And the thing was good in the eyes of Pharaoh, and in the eyes of all his servants. And Pharaoh said unto his servants, Can we find such a one as this is, a man in whom the Spirit of God is? And Pharaoh said unto Joseph, Forasmuch as God hath showed thee all this, there is none so discreet and wise as thou art: Thou shalt be over my house, and according unto thy word shall all my people be ruled: only in the throne will I be greater than thou. And Pharaoh said unto Joseph, See, I have set thee over all the land of Egypt. And Pharaoh took off his ring from his hand, and put it upon Joseph's hand, and arrayed him in vestures of fine linen, and put a gold chain about his neck; and he made him to ride in the second chariot which he had; and they cried before him, Bow the knee: and he made him ruler over all the land of Egypt.   —Genesis 41:33-43

It is believed that Joseph was thirty years old when he stood before Pharaoh. This would mean that thirteen years had rolled their course since Joseph was sold into slavery. We know very little about the treatment by his brethren at Dothan, the short period of honored service in the house of Potiphar brought to a sudden end by the cruel and wicked temptress, and then the incident with the baker and the butler in prison. The rest of the bitter trial was known only to God and Joseph. However, all this is now history, as far as Joseph is concerned. If he had known Rutherford's words he might have sung, "Now these all lie behind me. Oh, for a well-tuned harp!"

I often try to picture the despised and rejected man from the prison stepping up into the second chariot, the newly-elected Prime Minister of Egypt. Every trace of humiliation is now gone, and instead of bowing to the men of Egypt, they bow the knee to him. My eye catches his attire, for he now wears "the distinguished coat of honor," suited only to be worn by the one who filled the highest place in Egypt, apart from Pharaoh.

How significantly Joseph's coats have marked out the different epochs of his life's history. First, "the coat of many colors," covering those early happy years of boyhood in Jacob's home at Hebron. Second, "the servant's coat," that associated him with the house of Potiphar. He was stripped of the first coat, and it was used to deceive his old father, then the second is used to deceive Potiphar, for when he fled he left it in the hand of Potiphar's wife who had so wickedly tempted him to sin. This she used as evidence to convict the innocent, God-fearing lad, with the result Potiphar had him put into the king's prison. Third, he wore "the criminal's coat," that marked him out as a notable criminal though innocent. From the day he left home, the course seemed to be downward, step by step, until he reached the lowest possible rung of the ladder — "numbered with the transgressors."

As far as his early dreams were concerned, which showed him rising to the place of honor and great exaltation, there seems to be no possibility of them being fulfilled. Instead of "up," it was "down." The fourth coat—"the seer's coat"—is Joseph's as he stands before Pharaoh. He is recognized as God's wise man, in contrast to all the wise men and magicians of Egypt. There comes into my mind at this point First Corinthians 1:27-29: "God hath chosen the foolish things of the world to confound the wise; and God hath chosen the weak things of the world to confound the things which are mighty; and base things of the world, and things which are despised, hath God chosen, yea, and things which are not, to bring to nought things that are: that no flesh should glory in His presence."

The fifth coat is "the distinguished coat of honor." Think you the dreams of Hebron's vale would cry to Joseph now and exclaim, "This is the day; this is the day!" As far as the turn in the tide of circumstances was concerned, his day of greatness had arrived, but there was yet part of his dreams awaiting fulfillment. The bowing down of the sheaves of the field, and the obeisance of sun, moon and stars, had yet to come; but come it must, though to Joseph the road to it was all dark. Joseph was exalted, and called to the throne, because of his personal worth, and Mr. Knapp says, "All this is typical of the present exaltation of the Lord Jesus Christ. He who once was crucified is now glorified. He whom men once put upon a gibbet, has been placed by God upon His throne. Joseph was given his place of exaltation in Egypt purely on the ground of his personal worth and actual service rendered by him to the country and kingdom of Egypt."

What a lovely parallel to this we find in Philippians 2. Of course, since Christ excels Joseph in personal worth and service, He excels in his God-given position in exaltation and glory; for, "God hath highly exalted Him, and given Him a name which is above every name: that at the name of Jesus every knee should bow . . . and that every tongue should confess that Jesus Christ is Lord, to the glory of God the Father" (vv. 9-11). No one went so low as Christ, and no

75

one has gone so high. Paul tells the Ephesians: "He . . . ascended up far above all heavens, that He might fill all things" (Eph. 4:10). Peter says, "Jesus Christ: who is gone into heaven, and is on the right hand of God; angels and authorities and powers being made subject unto Him" (1 Peter 3:22).

As to Pharaoh's dreams, and their interpretation, the river he saw in his dream was the Nile, called "the river of Egypt." The seven fat cows were the seven years of plenty, the seven lean cows the seven years of famine. The seven ears in one stalk told of the bountiful harvest in the first period; the seven ears withered, thin and blighted with the east wind, devouring the seven good ears, told of the famine that would follow in the last period. Having made known the interpretation of the dreams, Joseph now advises Pharaoh what to do. He warns him of the coming danger and horrors of famine, and urges him to make suitable provision to meet it. Without fear or favor he told him the truth. He made it clear that after the time of rich and bountiful blessing, there would be sore and grievous famine.

Joseph being used to convey to Pharaoh the need to make preparation for the future emergency, directs us again to our Lord Jesus who is described in Revelation 3:14 as "the faithful and true witness." He in His ministry held back nothing. He unveiled the future in no uncertain way (Luke 16:19-31). On one occasion He drew back the curtain of the eternal world and showed us two men beyond the scene of time. Were they together? No, between them there was "a great gulf fixed." On earth there was a great difference in their position and environment. The one was rich, and, no doubt, moved in a high social circle, enjoying every luxury money could buy; the other was a poor beggar who lay at the rich man's gate, desiring the crumbs that fell from the magnate's table.

The incident related by the Lord goes to prove that

it was not their difference in this life that affected their eternal destiny; instead, it was their attitude to God and His Word, for it is plain that the rich man had no ear for Moses and the prophets. The warnings of God in these books were unheeded; he closed his ear to the message of salvation. In a word, he ruled God out of his life, and as a result Jesus says he died, "and in hell he lift up his eyes, being in torments."

In contrast to this, Jesus says, "And it came to pass that the beggar died, and was carried by the angels into Abraham's bosom." The fact that when the poor beggar died he went to the place of comfort and eternal bliss was proof that in life, despite his poverty and misery, he had given ear to the message of God, and like Abraham, he was justified by faith. A place in Heaven can be had on no other grounds. The rich man had to learn, as he suffered in the region of the lost, that his lot was to be that of eternal isolation and separation from God and Heaven, for between him and earth, and also Heaven, "there was a great gulf fixed."

As Joseph gave the two sides of the truth to Pharaoh, so did our blessed Lord. He spoke to men in the clearest terms about coming judgment and the way of salvation. Take, for instance, His words in John 5:24 — "Verily, verily, I say unto you, He that heareth My word, and believeth on Him that sent Me, hath everlasting life, and shall not come into condemnation [judgment]; but is passed from death unto life."

The message of God to Pharaoh was that there would be a time of rich harvest for seven years, and then a grievous famine, and it was his duty not to neglect the warning of God but begin immediately to make preparation against the dark day that lies ahead. Is not this exactly the same message God has for men today? In Acts 17:30, 31 we read, God "now commandeth all men everywhere to repent: because He hath appointed a day, in the which He will judge the world in righteousness by that man whom He hath ordained; whereof He hath given assurance unto all men, in that He hath raised Him from the dead." The Lord Jesus told the sinners of His day, ". . . except ye repent, ye shall all likewise perish" (Luke 13:5).

Calvary's sacrifice, and its acceptance by God, ushered in the day of grace, which may be called the day of harvest. It is the day when provision has been made in the Gospel message, which, if believed, will give the believing sinner "boldness in the day of judgment." He will have no fear of soul hunger in the day when the divine provision is withdrawn. Mark the solemn words of Amos the prophet, "Behold, the days come, saith the Lord God, that I will send a famine in the land, not a famine of bread, nor a thirst for water, but for hearing the words of the Lord: and they shall wander from sea to sea, and from the north even to the east, they shall run to and fro to seek the word of the Lord, and shall not find it" (Amos 8:11, 12).

What a tragedy! What a calamity! For a soul to lament, among the legions of the lost, "The harvest is past, the summer is ended, and [I am] not saved" (Jer. 8:20). Had Pharaoh not accepted God's message through Joseph, and acted accordingly, he would have had to face the horrors, death and destruction of a worldwide famine. O sinner, listen to God's warning word, "Behold, now is the accepted time; behold, now is the day of salvation" (II Cor. 6:2). Tomorrow you could be too late to receive God's provision!

CHAPTER 12

JOSEPH'S NEW NAME

Not only did Pharaoh promote Joseph to the place of great honor by giving him his ring, arraying him in fine linen, putting a chain of gold about his neck, making him to ride in the second chariot, and causing Egypt to bow the knee to him, but he also changed his name and called him Zaphnath-paaneah, and gave him as his wife Asenath, the daughter of Poti-pherah, priest of On. How significant the Egyptian meaning of this new name: "The Saviour of the world"! What a pointer this is to our Lord Jesus Christ! You remember, prior to His birth, it was told Joseph by the angel of the Lord, ". . . thou shalt call his name JESUS: for He shall save His people from their sins." The message to the shepherds was, "Unto you is born this day in the city of David a Saviour, which is Christ the Lord." What a name: JESUS — JEHOVAH THE SAVIOUR! It was the name "Jesus" they put above His cross. The hymn-writer put it beautifully when he wrote:

And when He hung upon the tree,
They wrote this name above Him,
That all might see the reason we
For evermore must love Him.

On the cross Christ accomplished His mighty saving work when He died "the Just for the unjust, that He might bring us to God" (1 Peter 3:18). It was there He settled forever sin's tremendous claim. It was there He opened up the way back to God. We sing with the children:

*There's a way back to God from the dark paths of
    sin,
There's a door that is opened, and you may go in;
At Calvary's cross is where you begin,
    When you come as a sinner to Jesus.*

Christians are reminded in the New Testament that not only has He saved us from the DOOM of our sins by having died in our place, but He lives in the presence of God to save us from the DOMINION of sin, right to the end of the road—"to the uttermost"; and at His coming He will save us out of the very DOMAIN of sin. Then we shall go to be where He is, in that realm of glory "where no shade nor stain can enter." Lift your heart to God now and thank Him for the Saviour. We have already seen from Philippians 2 that at the name of Jesus every knee must bow, in heaven, in earth, and under the earth, and every tongue confess that Jesus Christ is Lord to the glory of God the Father.

The Rabbis also attach to Joseph's new name: "The Revealer of Secrets," which, if right, shows us yet another way in which this new name typifies the Lord Jesus. Joseph, both in prison and now before Pharaoh, had shown himself as God's instrument to disclose the secrets locked up in the dreams of men. Paul says of the Lord Jesus in 1 Corinthians 4:5 that He is the One "Who both will bring to light the hidden things of darkness, and will make manifest the counsels of the hearts," and again in Romans 2:11-16: "For there is no respect of persons with God. . . . In the day when God shall judge the secrets of men by Jesus Christ according to my gospel." Our Lord Himself is heard saying in Luke 8:17: "For nothing is secret, that shall not be made manifest; neither any thing hid, that shall not be known and come to light." This surely is a

80

staggering thought, especially for the poor foolish sinner: to think that in the coming day of judgment, the Judge whom he must meet is One who will need no witnesses, for as Revelation 1:14 says, as John saw Him, "His eyes were as a flame of fire." Not even the secrets of the heart are beyond His gaze. The hymn-writer asks a solemn question:

> *What will you do in that great day*
> *When Heaven and earth shall pass away,*
> *When all your pomp and glory here*
> *Like morning dew shall disappear,*
> *And you from out your lonely tomb*
> *Shall stand in judgment's awful doom?*

CHAPTER 13

THE GENTILE BRIDE

We now consider Joseph in command of all Egypt, arrayed in garments of glory, wearing, shall we say, "the coat of honor," and united to Asenath. Thus we have a Hebrew linked with a Gentile bride, and though all may not agree, I feel we have a picture of Christ the Heavenly Bridegroom who in the day of His glory will be seen in association with His loved bride for whom He gave His life to make her His very own. This calls to mind the beautiful and familiar passage of Ephesians 5:22-33 in which we read: "Christ also loved the church, and gave Himself for it; that He might sanctify and cleanse it with the washing of water by the word, that He might present it to Himself a glorious church, not having spot, or wrinkle, or any such thing; but that it should be holy and without blemish" (vv. 25-27). This passage, in dealing with the marriage union, says in verse 32, "This is a great mystery: but I speak concerning Christ and the church." As the marriage bond joins man and wife and makes one flesh, so the church as the bride of Christ is joined to her Heavenly Bridegroom. Revelation 19:7 points to that coming day of gladness and rejoicing because it says, "The marriage of the Lamb is come, and His wife hath made herself ready."

C. I. Scofield in his note shows that the Oriental pattern of marriage covers three stages. First, the betrothal, legally binding — when the individual members of the body of Christ are saved. Second, the coming of the Bridegroom for the bride — this will take place at the Rapture, the coming of Christ for His church (1 Thess. 4:13, 14). Third, the marriage supper of the Lamb — occurring in connection with the second stage of Christ's coming to establish His millennial kingdom. As we think of the royal splendor and pageantry that would mark the union of Egypt's prime minister with Asenath, our minds take a rapid flight to that great "marriage of the Lamb" with its royal supper to which the blessed are called.

Revelation 19:7-9 describes the bride in that day: The "wife hath made herself ready. And to her was granted that she should be arrayed in fine linen, clean and white: for the fine linen is the righteousness [righteousnesses, marg.] of saints." Notice that the plural is used here, and it is simply practical righteousness that is referred to. It is how we live while here on earth that is going to determine how we will shine as individuals in that day.

William Hagan of Belfast, our departed and esteemed brother and teacher, once said, "Brethren, we shall only wear up there, what we weave down here." This terse statement gives the exact meaning of the passage, and surely calls for exercise of heart as to how the Christian is filling in the quickly passing days in service for the Master.

Before we return to Joseph let us note that prior to the marriage supper the Christian will have been made manifest at the judgment seat of Christ (2 Cor. 5:10). His life will have been gone into; he will have rendered the account of his stewardship. The extent of his reward will have been determined, and every man have had praise of God (1 Cor. 4:5). How solemn to think that based upon the findings of that vital interview will be decided our place in the coming kingdom of our Lord Jesus.

83

He is coming — oh! how solemn
When the Judge's voice is heard,
And in His own light He shows us
Every thought and act and word!
Deeds of merit as we thought them,
He will show us were but sin,
Little acts we had forgotten,
He will tell us were for Him.

Joseph, as the "lord of the land," goes throughout the land of Egypt gathering up the food of those plentiful years of which Pharaoh dreamed. What a gathering that was! Genesis 41:47-49 reads: "And in the seven plenteous years the earth brought forth by handfuls. And he gathered up all the food of the seven years, which were in the land of Egypt, and laid up the food in the cities: the food of the field, which was round about every city, laid he up in the same. And Joseph gathered corn as the sand of the sea, very much, until he left numbering; for it was without number."

As I think of Joseph making such wise preparation against the coming famine, I am reminded of the words of the wise man in Proverbs 6: "Go to the ant, thou sluggard; consider her ways, and be wise: which having no guide, overseer, or ruler, provideth her meat in the summer, and gathereth her food in the harvest" (vv. 6-8). Surely this emphasizes the point of dealing with provision for the future. The Lord would counsel the sinner to take a lesson from the wise little ant, seeing that the harvest of grace is passing and the summer of opportunity will soon be ended.

CHAPTER 14

THE SONS OF JOSEPH

Before the seven years of plenty had ended, Asenath bore Joseph two sons: the first was called Manasseh; the second, Ephraim. How significant are their names! Manasseh means "forgetting"; Ephraim means "fruitful." Joseph had them so named because he said as to the first, "God hath made me to FORGET all my toil, and all my father's house"; as to the second he said, "For God hath caused me to be FRUITFUL in the land of my affliction." You may wonder if Joseph could be so unnatural as to forget his father's house. This is not what he meant. He was thinking rather of the unkindness and cruel treatment of his brethren who robbed him of his "coat of many colors," and sold him into slavery, for as he looks back over the years to these days he could see the outworking of the divine plan. The fact that the names he gave to his two sons were Hebrew names tells us that he had not forgotten the sweet "vale of Hebron."

Although Joseph had no idea of what lay ahead of him he was prepared to take a step at a time and patiently await the gradual unfolding of the plan and purpose of his God. Again, in giving Ephraim the name which really means "double fruitfulness," he shows that he knew the firstborn's right to have a double portion of his father's inheritance. He did not give him a "coat of many colors" but he did give him a name which marked him out as the distinguished one who would fill "the first place."

Note also that Joseph still spoke of Egypt as "the land of his affliction." Egypt was not Hebron. He looked upon himself as a pilgrim and a stranger in a strange land. Again we are reminded of our blessed Lord whose life in this world, during the days of His flesh, was marked by toil, and affliction. He surely was a pilgrim and a stranger! He always had before Him that day when He would go back to His Father, but that way back for Him was via Calvary. Speaking of this in John 12:23, 24, He said, "The hour is come, that the Son of man should be glorified. Verily, verily, I say unto you, Except a corn of wheat fall into the ground and die, it abideth alone: but if it die, it bringeth forth MUCH FRUIT." Hebrews 2:13 pictures our Lord conducting the saved millions into His Father's presence, exclaiming, "Behold I and the children which God hath given Me." Then indeed shall be seen the meaning of the "much fruit."

> *The countless multitude on high*
> *That tune their song to Jesus' name,*
> *All merit of their own deny,*
> *And Jesus' worth alone proclaim.*
>
> *Firm on the ground of sovereign grace,*
> *They stand before Jehovah's throne,*
> *The only song in that blest place,*
> *Is, "Thou art worthy! Thou alone!"*

No doubt, in that coming day of glory, the words of the prophet will be true, and most blessedly realized by Him, "He shall see of the travail of His soul, and shall be satisfied" (Isa. 53:11).

CHAPTER 15

THE DAY OF PLENTY ENDS

And the seven years of plenteousness, that was in the land of Egypt, were ended. And the seven years of dearth began to come, according as Joseph had said: and the dearth was in all the lands; but in all the land of Egypt there was bread. And when all the land of Egypt was famished, the people cried to Pharaoh for bread: and Pharaoh said unto all the Egyptians, Go unto Joseph; what he saith to you, do. And the famine was over all the face of the earth: and Joseph opened all the storehouses, and sold unto the Egyptians; and the famine waxed sore in the land of Egypt.

—Genesis 41:53-56

Alas, the day has come — the day of famine! Now would be seen the wisdom of having prepared for the evil day. How glad and thankful Pharaoh and his people would be, that they had acted on Joseph's instructions! What a calamity it would have been had they neglected to make preparation in the golden years of bountiful harvest! Here again the warning must be pressed home to any who are unprepared to meet God. Remember, "Time is earnest passing by, death and judgment draweth nigh." Are the words of the old-time Gospel hymn true of you? —

> *Many summers you have wasted,*
> *Ripened harvests you have seen,*
> *Winter snows by spring have melted,*
> *Yet you linger in your sin.*

I plead with you to lay hold on God's provision in Christ. Look by faith to His cross, and rest on Christ's sin-atoning sacrifice. Do not delay; do it now.

How striking is Pharaoh's reply to the people when they cried to him for bread; they knew the storehouses were packed with abundant provision, but how was it to be obtained? That was the great question. "Go unto Joseph," answered Pharaoh. Was there no one else? There was no one else — Zaphnath-Paaneah was "the savior of the land." It was wonderful that the rejected Jew should be exalted into the place of a savior for a famine-smitten world, and that this rejected Jew should be the "only" savior.

Meditate on this and think of another rejected Jew— One of whom the prophet speaks as "despised and rejected of men" and again, "He was despised, and we esteemed Him not." It was our blessed Lord Jesus. One day Christ presented Himself to His nation as "The Bread of Life" (John 6:35). At this time many turned back and walked no more with Him. Then Christ looked on His own little band and said with pathos, "Will ye also go away?" to which Peter replied, "Lord, to whom shall we go?" and continued as if to say, "but UNTO THEE?" In John 14:6 Christ declares, "I am the way, the truth, and the life: no man cometh unto the Father but by Me." The word for the hungry sinner today is, "Go to Jesus." To be saved from the pangs of soul-hunger there is but one way of escape, and that is "Go to Jesus"; and go now for tomorrow could be too late.

The packed and crammed storehouses of Egypt, remind us of the bountifulness of Christ's provision for a starving world. In one of His miracles, recorded by each of the four gospelers, we see Him confronted by a multitude of thousands, and out of His hand coming a full supply from five loaves and two small fishes, after which they gathered up twelve baskets full of the fragments that remained. What a supplier! The amount of Joseph's provision could not be counted; we are told earlier in our story that it was "as the sand of the sea."

Thank God there is sufficient in Christ to meet the need of the whole wide world. First Timothy 2:6 reads, "He gave Himself a ransom for ALL."

There are many voices in the world today crying loudly to the sons of men, offering satisfaction to meet that aching void in the human soul. How many there are who have given ear and have followed in one direction or another seeking to find it! Some are tempted to follow the voice of worldly pleasure, worldly fame, or worldly wealth. But their only reward is sad disappointment. Lord Byron listened to the world's call; hear him one morning after a night of drinking deeply at the world's pleasure fount:

> *Though gay companions round the bowl,*
> *Dispel awhile the sense of ill,*
> *And pleasures fill the maddening soul,*
> *The heart—the heart, is lonely still.*

The aching void remained. What had he to say at the end of his life?

> *My days are in the yellow leaf,*
> *The flowers and fruits of earth are gone,*
> *The worm, the canker, and the grief*
> *Are mine alone.*

Millions have accepted God's provision in Christ, "The Bread of Life." What testimonies could be given of the satisfaction found in Him when all else had failed! One truly satisfied soul wrote one day:

> *I tried the broken cisterns, Lord,*
> *But, ah! the waters failed!*
> *E'en as I stooped to drink, they fled*
> *And mocked me as I wail'd.*

> *Now none but Christ can satisfy,*
> *None other name for me,*
> *There's love and life and lasting joy,*
> *Lord Jesus, found in Thee.*

89

CHAPTER 16

SAVIOUR OF THE LAND

Joseph opened all the storehouses and sold to the Egyptians. Pharaoh and Joseph made the Egyptians "buy" all the food they needed. But God's provision in Christ, to meet the need of a spiritually hungry world, is offered to "whosoever will" accept it, without money, and without price. Isaiah the prophet cries, "Ho, every one that thirsteth, come ye to the waters, and he that hath no money; come ye, buy, and eat; yea, come, buy wine and milk without money and without price. Wherefore do ye spend money for that which is not bread? and your labour for that which satisfieth not? hearken diligently unto me, and eat that which is good, and let your soul delight itself in fatness" (55:1, 2).

While this is blessedly true, there is a sense in which the sinner has a price to pay to obtain salvation. Indeed this is why so many who may have learned their need of being saved "halt between two opinions" and eventually turn away and refuse the Divine provision in Christ to meet their needs, thus failing to make their Heaven sure. The one who would really accept Christ must be absolutely clear on this point: that a price has to be paid. Listen to His words in Luke 9:23 as the multitude hung upon His words. "And He said to them all, If any man will come after Me, let him deny himself, and take up his cross daily, and follow Me. For whosoever will save his life shall lose it: but whosoever will lose his life for My sake, the same shall save it." In John 6 we read that when Christ did press home His claims to the would-be disciples ". . . many went back and walked no more with Him." A choice has to be made. If salvation is going to be obtained it means good-bye to a life of sinful pleasure, separation from a Godless society, to share in the reproach of a rejected Christ. Moses did exactly that. It is said of him, he "refused to be called the son of Pharaoh's daughter; choosing rather to suffer affliction with the people of God, than to enjoy the pleasures of sin for a season; esteeming the reproach of Christ greater riches than the treasures in Egypt: for he had respect unto the recompence of the reward" (Heb. 11:24-26). When Christ puts forth His claims in Luke 9 He then throws out the challenging question, "For what is a man advantaged, if he gain the whole world, and lose himself?"

The famine in Egypt was so widespread and universal, that we read, "And all countries came into Egypt to Joseph for to buy corn; because that the famine was so sore in all lands" (Gen. 41:57). "All countries came into Egypt to Joseph"; there was but one place, and one person. It was vain to seek elsewhere, for Joseph was the one and only "saviour of the land." Here I just want to emphasize the importance of grasping this point in God's universal plan to meet a world's need, that every seeking sinner must come to the one place, Calvary, and to the one person, Christ — and only Christ. He is the key to the whole situation.

Having now reached Genesis 42 we come to the last and final step of Joseph's exaltation, and to the many strange incidents which mark the gradual progress of that forward movement before the ultimate stage is reached. The closing eight chapters of the book are reserved for the unfolding of the fascinating episode that has charmed millions of Bible readers through the years. It is a story that grips the child and causes him to open his eyes wide at poor little Benjamin, filled with confusion, as the lord of Egypt's silver cup is found in his sack. On the other hand the interested Bible student digs into every page of the story, finding here a mine of precious ore. Is he looking for types? He finds them here. Is he looking for principles? He finds them here. Is he looking for sections which abound with practical lessons? He finds them here. Is he looking for illustrations for his exposition of divine truth? He finds these precious pages brim full of the same. To the Holy Spirit-taught Christian these eight chapters are indeed a mine of wealth, apart from being a classic in literature. Shall we proceed to dig for some of the precious gold?

CHAPTER 17

THE BRETHREN GO TO EGYPT

Genesis 42 records the first meeting of Joseph with his brethren since that day they stripped him of his "coat of many colors" and sold him into slavery. More than twenty years had rolled by. He is not now the gentle stripling as they knew him in Hebron's vale. He is the stately lord of Egypt approaching the mature age of forty. His regalia is that of a mighty prince. To all intents and purposes he is as Pharaoh apart from the throne. It is as such his brethren must meet him. Poor old mourning Jacob now comes into the picture. This is the first mention of him since we left him gazing on the "coat of many colors" saturated with blood, brokenhearted and refusing to be comforted.

Now Jacob is in the grip of famine. Food supplies for the large family are fast diminishing. His grown sons are getting to be at wit's end corner, and all they can do is to "look one upon another" wondering what to do, or where to go, for their case was really becoming desperate. It is here the old patriarch, Israel, rises as the man of faith. Look how the passage begins: "Now when Jacob saw that there was corn in Egypt [evidently others had been to Egypt and had brought back corn for their houses], Jacob said unto his sons, . . . Behold, I have heard that there is corn in Egypt." Surely this is faith's principle. Romans 10 declares, "Faith cometh by hearing." It is said of Moses ". . . he endured, as seeing Him who is invisible."

93

Naturally Jacob couldn't see the storehouses, but he was prepared to act on what he heard.

This is exactly how a soul gets saved. Natural eyes cannot look back almost two thousand years to see a suffering Saviour hanging on the tree of shame, bearing "our sins in His own body on the tree" (1 Peter 2:24). No, but what the sinner can do is open his ear to the Word of God, yea, to the very word of Christ Himself: ". . . even so must the Son of man be lifted up: that whosoever believeth in Him should not perish, but have eternal life." To BELIEVE is simply to LOOK. Look by the eye of faith to the uplifted Saviour and rest on His finished work. "Without faith it is impossible to please [God]" (Heb. 11:6). Noah, who SAW the flood coming — not with his natural eye, but he had God's word that it would come — opened his ear to God, believed His word, and built an ark to the saving of his house. All who failed to believe God's word and warning perished in the waters of judgment.

We can judge that things were in a very serious state with Jacob and the families at Hebron, for he says to his sons, ". . . get you down thither, and buy for us [corn] from thence; that we may live, and not die." It was a matter of life or death. To sit where they were and make no effort would certainly mean starving to death. There was corn in Egypt, but the effort had to be made to get there, and money had to be taken to pay for corn. It is so with the sons of men today. There is provision to meet the sinner's need. Christ is presented in the Gospel as the One who can satisfy every longing of the human heart, but as it was in Egypt, every seeker after corn got the message, "GO TO JOSEPH," so in the Gospel today the message for the sinner is, "GO TO JESUS." You see, it is as Scripture says, we must make an effort to go where the provision is to be found, and be prepared to buy it. It is indeed a matter of life or death. In your soul's hunger, sinner, make an effort to "Go to Jesus," and there you will find "eternal life." If you sit where you are, unconcerned, and giving no thought to the eternal famine lying ahead, when there will be no "Bread of Life" to be obtained, then perish you must, and that eternally. Those of us who have given heed to the Gospel call and responded to Christ's loving invitation, can look up into His face and say, "Satisfied with Thee, Lord Jesus, I am blessed." To those who believe in Him, He says, "He that believeth in Me shall never die" (John 11:26).

We now picture these ten men, money in hand, saying good-bye to their families and setting out on the long trek to the land of Egypt. I wonder what their thoughts would be! Year after year they had been watching their old father in his continual mourning for his long lost son. How often in the past would conscience have recalled with its bitter sting that day when they stripped Joseph of his "coat of many colors," and despite the anguish of his soul, handed him over to the slave traders! Surely it was impossible for them not to be haunted with fears of divine retribution. For all they knew, death might have ended the career of the innocent lad, and if that were so, then God would require his blood at their hand. Why did they so treat him? Had he hurt them or wronged them in any way? No indeed! Was it not on the very occasion of his long journey to seek their welfare that they so vilely and cruelly treated him. The answer is: It was nothing but envy and sheer jealousy that caused them to act so wickedly. You remember when they had decided to get him out of the way how they said, "And we shall see what will become of his dreams."

My thoughts are carried over to Another who was so treated. In Mark 15:9 Pilate asked the multitude, "Will ye that I release unto you the King of the Jews?" This he really desired to do "for he knew that the chief

95

priests had delivered Him for ENVY." Those dreams of Joseph pointing forward to a day of exaltation, were more than his brethren could accept or think possible, and this caused them to be filled with envy and the desire to get rid of him. It was so with our blessed Lord when He stood before the high priest. "And the high priest stood up in the midst, and asked Jesus, . . . What is it which these witness against Thee? But He held His peace, and answered nothing. Again the high priest asked Him, and said unto Him, Art Thou the Christ, the Son of the Blessed? And Jesus said, I am: and ye shall see the Son of man sitting on the right hand of power, and coming in the clouds of heaven. Then the high priest rent his clothes, and saith, What need we any further witnesses? Ye have heard the blasphemy: what think ye? And they all condemned Him to be guilty of death" (Mark 14:60-64).

They could not bear to think of Jesus the Nazarene "sitting on the right hand of power, and coming in the clouds of heaven," hence, filled with envy they handed Him over to a malefactor's death with all its attendant ignominy and shame. Had He hurt them in any way? Did He ever wrong them or harm them? Nay, verily, He came to seek them, when they were lost; He came to bring them salvation. The Holy Spirit's testimony regarding His sojourn in this scene was, "He went about doing good" (Acts 10:38). There is a sense in which Joseph by his God-fearing life and conduct showed up the wickedness of his brethren, for only wicked men could act as they had done. This is exactly what marked the life of Christ as He moved in and out amongst men and especially among the religious leaders of that day. He stood in their presence, "holy, harmless, undefiled" (Heb. 7:26), and this but made their own wicked, hypocritical acting stand out the more in bold relief and stare them in the very face, until they could not abide His presence. This explains why they continually dogged His steps, tried to catch Him in His words, and eventually engineered the plot to get rid of Him.

Has God forgotten their wicked treatment and rejection of His blessed, sinless Son? By no means. At Calvary they gave the fullest possible demonstration of the wickedness and the hatred that was in their hearts, even though Pilate had washed his hands and said, "I am innocent of the blood of this just person, see ye to it" (Matt. 27:24). All the people answered, "His blood be on us, and on our children." During the last centuries what a tale could be told of the sufferings, persecutions and wholesale massacres that have befallen the guilty nation as the result of their bloodguiltiness in crucifying their heaven-sent Messiah. Who can tell what has yet to be endured in "the great tribulation" that is yet to come!

Before proceeding let us learn a lesson here as the children of God. Peter, in his first letter, addressing "born again ones," says, "Wherefore having laid aside all malice, and all guile, and hypocrisies, and envies, and all evil speakings, as newborn babes, desire the sincere milk of the word, that ye may grow thereby" (2:1-2). Note that the propelling force behind the brethren's treatment of their brother was envy, and in the case of our blessed Lord it was exactly the same. But Peter reminds us that the Christian is looked upon as having laid this aside, and the force of the word is the casting off of an old garment, never to be put on again. The wise man reminds us that "Jealousy is as cruel as the grave" (Song of Sol. 8:6). The Lord enable us to deal with this cruel vice, so that by the power of the indwelling Spirit, it shall be expelled from our lives, and especially in the treatment of our fellow Christians.

Earlier we were wondering what would be the thoughts of Joseph's brethren as they set out for Egypt to buy bread, the vale of Hebron being gripped by the famine. From this point on, the story seems to fit in piece by piece so naturally, and yet the supernatural is also evident. One can see that every turn of the wheels concerning God's plan and purpose from Joseph's birth into this world right through to his death and burial in Canaan regulated all the events that go to make up this fascinating story. Yes indeed, we fully agree with the great Cowper:

> *God moves in a mysterious way,*
> *His wonders to perform;*
> *He plants His footsteps in the sea,*
> *And rides upon the storm.*
>
> *Deep in unfathomable mines*
> *Of never failing skill,*
> *He treasures up His bright designs,*
> *And works His Sovereign will.*

CHAPTER 18

THE JOURNEY BACK

It is very touching to read concerning the brethren's departure: "But Benjamin, Joseph's brother, Jacob sent not with his brethren: for he said, Lest peradventure mischief befall him" (Gen. 42:4). Was his mind traveling back to the day he sent out Joseph to seek the welfare of his brethren? His brethren should have seen to it that no evil befell him. How dreadful if he should let Benjamin go with them and some calamity overtake him, and he would never return! I believe this is what old Jacob was afraid of and so he decided that Benjamin would stay by his side. Yet before obtaining more corn, and when it was a matter of life or death, Jacob had to learn that to receive the full blessing lying in store for him he would have to part with Benjamin and leave the result in God's hand. (More of this when we reach the point when Jacob must make the vital decision.)

We do not know what happened on the way as the brethren journeyed to buy the corn for their houses, for Scripture is silent on the matter. I cannot but feel they had their fears, for no doubt the sting of conscience was continually smarting. Was it warning them that "God requireth that which is past"? Did they think of their child brother whom they had sent on this very road so long ago? Were they gazing at the skeleton in the cupboard? Of course with the spirit of adventure gripping them, and to think they were going to see the great land of the Nile and the big outside world of which until now they had known little, this would no doubt give them subject material to occupy their minds and help them in some measure at least to forget the past with its haunting memories. Little did they know that every step was taking them nearer to meeting the one against whom they had so grievously sinned.

A guilty conscience is a bad companion; it is that silent monitor, put within man by the Creator God, which tells the sinner as with a thousand voices, "That was a dark deed! That was wrong! That was sin against God!" Its voice will not be silenced. It thunders home in threatening tones the fact of coming judgment, when the criminal act so long ago committed will have to be faced before the righteous Judge "whose eyes are as a flame of fire" (Rev. 1:14).

The Apostle Paul had a deep exercise about having a "conscience void of offence toward God, and toward men." To his son Timothy he stresses the value of a good conscience and a pure conscience, and on the other hand the grave danger of being so accustomed to sin as to develop a seared conscience, a conscience which becomes insensitive, having lost its restraining and convicting power. Pity the saint, or sinner, whoever he may be that allows a tender conscience to become seared, so that the warning voice is silent and sin no longer appears to be sin. Certainly the Christian who fails to keep a tender conscience can only expect that the link of communion with his God is sure to snap, and that he himself must come under the chastening rod — "For whom the Lord loveth He chasteneth" (Heb. 12:6).

John tells us in his first letter that "Whosoever is born of God doth not commit [does not practise] sin" (1 John 3:9). For this we judge that a person who claims to be a Christian and can go on sinning and have no conscience about it has never been born again and has only a mere empty profession, which in the end will leave him on the wrong side of Heaven's door.

The brethren's journey completed, they find themselves among the seething crowds, for from all countries they came to Egypt to buy corn. What a change of environment from tending the sheep in the homeland! We go with them into the distribution center where the officials, under Joseph's supervision, were selling the precious grain. No doubt they were quick to see that they could not expect to receive any special favors, even though they belonged to a notable and distinguished family. If they had any thoughts along this line, they soon vanished, for all that came were on the same level and were treated alike. There was no respect of persons. The same principle marks the handing out of God's provision today. Those who come to Christ for salvation find how true this is. It matters not the color, class or creed, be it Jew or Gentile, bond or free, everyone is received on one common ground.

How beautifully this is displayed in the Lord's dealings with sinners while He was here! In John 3 He is bringing salvation and the gift of eternal life to a Jewish ruler, a notable Pharisee and member of the Jewish Council. In the following chapter He is sitting by Sychar's well, deep in conversation with a Samaritan woman who had come to draw water from the well. I remember a preacher speaking of her as "a woman who had written her past in very black ink." The story at least would tell us that she had a hungry and thirsty soul which the manner of her life in the past had failed to satisfy. To such an one Jesus brings salvation. He gave her a drink of "the living water." This quenched her spiritual thirst and sent her away with the word to the men of the city, "Come, see a man, which told me all things that ever I did: is not this the Christ?" (John 4:29). Another day He receives a wealthy tax gatherer

101

and gives him the blessing of salvation, and yet only a little time before He was called, we find Jesus stopping the crowd to allow a poor blind beggar the opportunity of receiving his sight and with it the gift of salvation.

I remember hearing the late Mr. Harold St. John tell of being in Miss Habershon's guest house before the First World War. While there he went for a long walk in the country during which he met a beggar who asked for help. The saintly man was quick to respond, and then he asked the poor man to sit down on the roadside for a little talk. The precious moments were filled presenting the Gospel message to a most interested listener. When this was over Mr. St. John gave him some Gospel tracts to read, and they parted likely never to meet again. On returning he found Miss Habershon had received one of the Balkan kings and his queen. She asked Mr. St. John if he would like to meet the monarch. He said he would be delighted. So she introduced them and they went out to the balcony to have a talk. Again the soul winner got to work, and before long the king was having poured into his ear the blessed Gospel message. He also gave him some Gospel tracts in a suitable language. When the interview was over Mr. St. John returned to Miss Habershon saying, "Thank God the message that suited the beggar on the roadside suited the king on the balcony."

Another illustration of the precious truth that God is no respecter of persons, takes us to a church in Manchester, England, where Harry Moorhouse, the great evangelist, was preaching. One night at the end of the service a titled lady was found sitting in the gallery after all the others had gone. She was anxious to be saved and was waiting to see the little preacher. As he came to her side and she made known her earnest desire to find salvation, he happened to look across the gallery, and there he saw a Christian worker talking to a poor disheveled street-walker who was seeking the same blessing. He drew the lady's attention to her and said, "Would you go across and together make your way to the Saviour?" With no thought of her station in life, she immediately arose and rushed across the gallery, threw her arms around the profligate's neck, and together they wept their way to the Saviour. This is exactly how Peter introduced the Roman centurion Cornelius to the terms upon which he could receive salvation. He began by saying, "Of a truth I perceive that God is no respecter of persons" (Acts 10:34). In the previous chapters it was a dark-skinned Ethiopian who obtained this blessing, followed by a young Jewish theologian student, and here it is a Roman soldier.

Let John 3:16 fill our vision ere we leave this precious theme: "For God so loved the world, that He gave His only begotten Son, that WHOSOEVER believeth in Him should not perish, but have everlasting life."

CHAPTER 19

MEETING THE LORD OF THE LAND

What a surprise for Joseph's brethren when making their purchase! They found themselves confronted by "the lord of the land." By this time they would have heard of his fame, for no doubt he would be talked about by the crowds who thronged the storehouses. Look at them as they find themselves in the presence of the mighty and dignified Egyptian. What else could they do but as the Orientals do in the presence of a royal personage? They bring their foreheads to the ground, and before resuming an erect position either kiss the earth or the feet or border of the garment of the standing dignitary. This the brethren did. I will not even try to describe what the inner feelings were in the heart of Joseph as he watched these ageing men get down and kiss the very ground upon which he stood. We read, "And Joseph knew his brethren, but they knew not him. And Joseph remembered the dreams" (Gen. 42:8, 9).

Ah, in memory he was back in the field where he saw his sheaf standing, and where he saw his brothers' sheaves bowing down to him! Was not this a splendid opportunity to bring those wicked men to their knees and bring out to the light their hidden past and send word back to his father that the blood-stained "coat of many colors" was a cruel and wicked trick to cover up their foul deed at Dothan? We might say this is just what they deserved; they had a right to reap what they had sown. Had they not been already reaping? What about those haunting twenty years — daily fearing the avenging hand of God? Conscience, as we have seen, was continually harrowing their feelings, and the sobs and tears of their old father were cutting them to the quick as he mourned for his loved son. Yes, they had been reaping. We must never forget Galatians 6:7 — "Be not deceived; God is not mocked: for whatsoever a man soweth, that shall he also reap." This is a Divine principle that has never varied in the past and will know no change in the future.

The God-fearing Joseph is now seeing the unfolding of the Divine plan. He can see plainly how the hand of God had been guiding through the maze of the past years since he left the vale of Hebron. Surely he would recall the stripping from him of his "coat of many colors," the horrible pit, the Ishmeelite caravan, Potiphar's house, the wicked woman who tried to ruin him, the prison where "the iron entered his soul," the baker and the butler with their dreams, the long weary years of isolation, the dreams of Pharaoh, the failure of the wise men of Egypt to interpret the same, the revelation given him by God of the years of plenty and following them years of famine, and the unexpected rise to worldwide fame.

However, the time was not yet come for Joseph to disclose his identity, so he sets out in the execution of a seemingly strange plan, and yet not strange when we remember that Joseph was anxious to find out about conditions in Hebron. Would his father be living or dead? And what about little Benjamin? Had his brethren known any change of heart? Was there any repenting of the wrong they had done him? All this would be brought out in the course of his dealings with his brethren in the chapters that follow.

It is plain to see that Joseph, having recognized the hand of God guiding over the past years for a Divine purpose, had no desire for revenge, no desire to pay

105

back his brethren in their own coin. No, his heart was soft toward them, and he only longed for the moment to arrive when he could make himself known to them and eventually bring them into the land of plenty.

Was not this the attitude of God toward us? Psalm 103:10 and 11 says, "He hath not dealt with us after our sins; nor rewarded us according to our iniquities. For as the heaven is high above the earth, so great is His mercy toward them that fear Him." Paul's word to the Romans is lovely in this connection: "For when we were yet without strength, in due time Christ died for the ungodly. For scarcely for a righteous man will one die: yet peradventure for a good man some would even dare to die. But God commendeth His love toward us, in that, while we were yet sinners, Christ died for us" (5: 6-8). Again, to Titus Paul writes: "But after that the kindness and love of God our Saviour toward man appeared, not by works of righteousness which we have done, but according to His mercy He saved us, by the washing of regeneration, and renewing of the Holy Ghost; which He shed on us abundantly through Jesus Christ our Saviour" (3: 4-6).

Though it was true that Joseph's brethren had grievously wronged him, yet it was in his heart to bless them. The question of merit did not arise, and it was well for them because they had none to plead.

CHAPTER 20

THE UNEXPECTED INTERROGATION

Let us now see the attitude Joseph adopted toward his brethren. The record says, ". . . he knew them, but made himself strange unto them, and spake roughly unto them." He at once began dealing with them in this manner in view of leading them to repentance and eventually to bring them into the good of reconciliation. This is the way the Lord so often deals with sinners, especially those who come before Him in their self-righteousness. How hard it is for them to hear the prophet's words in Isaiah 64:6, "But we are all as an unclean thing, and all our righteousnesses are as filthy rags"! How many there are who rest upon good works to merit salvation and a place in Heaven! To them Ephesians 2:8 and 9 comes with force, "By grace are ye saved through faith; and that not of yourselves: it is the gift of God: not of works, lest any man should boast." For the sinner to be told that he can do absolutely nothing to effect his own salvation, and that despite his fancied goodness he "must be born again," and that he must be saved in the very same way as the vilest sinner, is indeed hard for him to accept. Yet this is God's way. The sinner must be made to feel his deep and dire need, be made to see his absolute unworthiness of receiving blessing from God, and be prepared to accept salvation as the gift of God, and all of grace. A. M. Toplady's words for the seeking sinner are lovely:

Nothing in my hand I bring,
Simply to Thy cross I cling;
Naked, come to Thee for dress;
Helpless, look to Thee for grace;
Foul, I to the fountain fly;
Wash me, Saviour, or I die!

Not the labour of my hands
Can fulfil Thy law's demands;
Could my zeal no respite know,
Could my tears forever flow,
All for sin could not atone;
Thou must save, and Thou alone.

Yes, Joseph spoke roughly to his brothers; he meant to probe deep, and to find out what was in their hearts. He begins with a serious accusation: "Whence come ye?" And they replied, "From the land of Canaan to buy food." And he said unto them, "Ye are spies; to see the nakedness of the land ye are come." One wonders why they had not eyes to see how ridiculous was his accusation. Who would send out ten men of one family to jeopardize their lives as spies? This would be far removed from the technique of secret intelligence methods. Anyhow they make their protest saying, "Nay, my lord, but to buy food are thy servants come." They do now what they never intended to do—they call him "lord," and take their place as his servants. Surely at that moment Joseph remembered his dreams. Then they went on, "We are all one man's sons"; and (as we would say) they put their foot in it, for they added, "We are TRUE men, thy servants are no spies." True men! Had they only known to whom they were speaking, such words never would have escaped their lips.

How Joseph would measure up this statement in the light of their past wickedness and deceit! How readily he could see the need for probing yet deeper, to bring them out in their true colors! Joseph could see by this description of themselves as "true men" that they were defending themselves, because of his accusation. It was true they were not spies, and well he knew that. But, as Joseph thought of the past and their wicked treatment of him, also the fact that their consciences without doubt would be harassing them over the years and telling them they were anything but true men, he felt he must continue to act in such a way as would convince them of their guilt. After that, he could assure them of his forgiveness and his purpose to bring them into the place of blessing.

What a picture of the nation of Israel are Joseph's brothers! Going back to the days in Jacob's home when Joseph was among them, he was the loved son of the father, distinguished as the firstborn, wearing his beautiful "coat of many colors." It was then they were filled with envy, despised him, rejected him and finally sold him into slavery. As far as they were concerned, and as far as poor old Jacob was concerned, Joseph was dead. We have now reached the day when these very men are driven out of their own land and find themselves in Egypt. Is not this exactly what happened to the nation of Israel when our blessed Lord came to them, the true Firstborn and loved Son of the Father? John tells us "He came unto His own, and His own received Him not" (John 1:11). No, they rejected Him, they cast Him out, and He was sold by the New Testament Judas, and finally crucified and slain.

What was the result? By A.D. 70 their land had been invaded by Titus and his armies, their city and Temple reduced to rubble, and they themselves driven out and scattered across the face of the earth. And as the brothers of Joseph had to know a gruelling experience before their eyes were opened to recognize "the lord of the land" as their very own Joseph, the

109

one whom they despised and rejected, so it will be with Israel. From the day they crucified their Messiah, from the day they cried, "This is the heir, come, let us kill him," until this very day, they have known the sorrows of a nation rejected by God, persecuted and despised, yea, a byword among the nations of the world, and in this condition they must remain until "they look upon Him whom they have pierced" when He returns as "King of kings, and Lord of lords."

In this interview Joseph continues to accuse them, despite their protest. He says, "Nay, but to see the nakedness of the land ye are come." This draws out from them another piece of information that Joseph was most anxious to have. They say to him, "Thy servants are twelve brethren, the sons of one man in the land of Canaan; and, behold, the youngest is this day with our father, AND ONE IS NOT" (Gen. 42:13). Now Joseph knows that his old father is still alive and that Benjamin is safe in the vale of Hebron, but they did not admit to the fact that they had sold the other one years ago as a slave. No, they cover up their crime by the vague expression, "and one is not."

What confusion would have filled them if at that moment he had said, "I am Joseph"! The time for that is not yet — there had to be more heart-searching before the time was ripe. Again Joseph accuses them, " That is that I spake unto you, saying, Ye are spies: hereby ye shall be proved: By the life of Pharaoh ye shall not go forth hence, except your youngest brother come hither. Send one of you, and let him fetch your brother, and ye shall be kept in prison, that your words may be proved, whether there be any truth in you: or else by the life of Pharaoh surely ye are spies. And he put them all together into ward three days" (42:14-17).

Perhaps it was into the very place where Joseph had been all these weary years. He would give them a

little taste of what it meant to be put into prison falsely accused. What a three days that was! Conscience
was lashing them without mercy. They were haunted
with that awful skeleton in the cupboard. In their
minds they were far away from Egypt. They were
back at Dothan and the shrieks and cries of a terrified
Joseph was thundering on the ears of their souls.
They say one to another, "We are verily guilty concerning our brother, in that we saw the anguish of his
soul, when he besought us, and we would not hear;
therefore is this distress come upon us. And Reuben
answered them saying, Spake I not unto you, saying,
Do not sin against the child; and ye would not hear?
therefore, behold, also his blood is required" (vv. 21-
22).

As Joseph heard the harrowing words of confession,
declaring their guilt in the shameful treatment they
had meted out to him, he would go back in mind to
that day, and would recall the anguish of his soul; he
would see how they had been living in continual dread
of Divine retribution. It was more than he could
bear, and so we read, "He turned himself about from
them, and wept." Well it was for them that they knew
not that Joseph understood them, for he spoke to
them by an interpreter.

On the third day Joseph said unto them, "This
do, and live; for I fear God: If ye be true men, let
one of your brethren be bound in the house of your
prison: go ye, carry corn for the famine of your
houses: but bring your youngest brother unto me; so
shall your words be verified, and ye shall not die"
(Gen. 42:18-20).

Looking at this episode I seem to hear the words of
Proverbs 13:15, "The way of transgressors is hard."
The fact that an Egyptian lord should cover his treatment of them with these words, "This do, and live,
for I fear God," must have been a severe rebuke to

111

them as it showed up the fact that when they so treated their innocent brother this is what they lacked. Had the fear of God been in their hearts they never would have acted as they did. The fear of God is a great safeguard. It was this that preserved Joseph from yielding to that sinful temptation in the house of Potiphar. And here I am reminded of Nehemiah who, when his fellow-rulers were acting wrongly in oppressing the people, said to them, "It is not good that ye do: ought ye not to walk in the fear of our God because of the reproach of the heathen our enemies?" (Neh. 5:9). His own conduct was different, and the reason is plain for he says, "But so did not I, because of the fear of God" (v. 15). It was a good old Irish saint who said, "Fear God and you have nobody else to fear."

How many a backsliding Christian, because of the lack of the fear of God, has wandered into by-paths, and as the result has fallen, proves indeed that "the way of transgressors is hard." But is it not beautiful to see how Joseph was touched at the sorry plight of his brothers, when he had to turn aside and weep to relieve his feelings? Any probing he would do and any heart searching he would engage in was all for the purpose of bringing them to repentance, and to eventually lead them back into his loving embrace. Mr. Moody was asked one day by a backslider, "What will God do with a Christian who has turned his back on Him?" The preacher's answer was short but sweet, "God will shine on his back," meaning of course that as soon as the offender would turn he would immediately be in the sunshine of the presence of God, forgiven and restored.

> *Though I forget Him and wander away,*
> *Still He doth love me wherever I stray,*
> *Back to His dear loving arms do I flee,*
> *When I remember that Jesus loves me.*

When recalling the case of Peter's denial and those bitter tears of sorrow and repentance, because of his incredible action in failing to own his link with the Saviour, we are made to see the sympathy and compassion of the One whom he had wronged. Did the gracious Lord turn His back on poor, failing Peter? Did He leave him to sink into a state of utter despair for weeks and months? By no means! On the very day He rose from the tomb, somewhere alone He had a meeting with Peter. The two who returned from Emmaus could tell the disciples in Jerusalem that "The Lord is risen indeed, and hath appeared to Simon." In 1 Corinthians 15:5 the first word Paul writes after mentioning the fact of the Lord's resurrection is, "He was seen of Cephas, then of the twelve." Peter first. The Good Shepherd had found His straying sheep. Yes, bless God, Peter was not only restored, but charged to strengthen his brethren and to feed the flock of God.

We have already quoted Joseph's instructions in verses 18-20. He would retain Simeon as a hostage while they would carry corn for their houses and return again bringing their youngest brother with them. Knowing them as he did, would you not be inclined to ask why did he not bind Reuben? He was the oldest, and no doubt the one whom Jacob held responsible for the safety of Joseph in that bygone day. Should he not have been made to suffer this imprisonment instead of Simeon? I think this could be the reason: Reuben was the one who prevented the brothers from taking Joseph's life, and who also planned to have him restored to his father. This Joseph learned, as Reuben blamed his brethren for their cruel and heartless treatment of the child, as being the cause for their present distress. Simeon was the second oldest, so Joseph bound him. The position now was this: if they should fail to bring their young-

113

est brother, then Simeon must remain in bonds. The principle was "A life for a life."

Can we not see here the idea of substitution? Is not this how every sinner finds salvation and eternal blessing, as by faith he takes his station at the foot of Calvary's tree? There he sees that Blessed One dying in his stead, surrendering His precious life, suffering the penalty due to the sinner's sin, and by accepting Christ as his Substitute immediately becomes the possessor of eternal life.

> *He took the guilty sinner's place,*
> *And suffered in his stead,*
> *For man, O miracle of grace,*
> *For man the Saviour bled.*

This is the blessed message of the Gospel.

Having taken Simeon and bound him before their eyes, Joseph commands his steward to fill their sacks with corn and to restore every man's money into his sack and to give them provision for the way. Then we read, "They laded their asses and departed." I remember our late brother Mr. William Gilmore preaching the Gospel to advantage from this passage. Speaking of Joseph's provision, he said, "Firstly, it was full, for he said, 'Fill their sacks'; secondly, it was free, for their money was restored; thirdly, it was lasting, for it was adequate to cover the needs of the whole journey home." How true this is about the salvation Jesus procured for the believing sinner, indeed, for the whole world, if they would but lay hold of it. There is a fullness in Christ to fill the aching void of the human heart and it is received without money and without price. It gives daily enjoyment and satisfaction "till the last step is taken, and Heaven is reached."

The writer to the Hebrews describes it as a "great salvation" and asks the question, "How shall we escape, if we neglect so great salvation?" (Heb. 2:3).

CHAPTER 21

THE HOMEWARD JOURNEY

Let us now follow the men on their homeward journey until they reach their first stopping place, where one of the men, on opening his sack to give his ass provender, found his purchasing money in his sack's mouth. And he said unto his brethren, "My money is restored; and lo it is even in my sack." And their hearts failed them, and they were afraid, saying one to another, "What is this that God hath done unto us?" This unexpected turn of events helped only to deepen the existing terror that had gripped them since first they were interrogated by the lord of the land. How were they to know that they would not be followed and overtaken and charged with stealing?

They were to learn, on their return visit with Benjamin, that it was the intention of the lord of the land that they should receive the provision as a gift from his bountiful hand. That is why their money was returned. How this points to the way in which our blessed Lord dispenses the blessing of salvation! As we have already noticed He hands it out freely. Paul terms it the "gift of God" in Romans 6:23 — "For the wages of sin is death, but the gift of God is eternal life through Jesus Christ our Lord." Our blessed Lord Himself, when talking to the woman of Samaria in John 4:10 said to her, "If thou knewest the gift of God, and who it is that saith to thee, Give me to drink; thou wouldest have asked of Him, and He would have given thee living water." Yes, salvation is the "gift of God," and "not of works lest any man should boast."

However, do not forget the vast amount of work that was needed to fill all those storehouses in order that the demands of a worldwide famine might be met. This directs us to the mighty work our blessed Saviour undertook in order to provide salvation for a world of sinners, lost and ruined by the Fall. True, it is offered and handed out as a free gift to "whosoever will," but what a cost to procure it! It is impossible for the mind of man to comprehend what Calvary meant to the Saviour. How terrible were His sufferings at the hands of His cruel tormentors, but oh, who could plumb the depths of those unfathomable seas of wrath when He cried out, "All Thy waves and Thy billows are gone over Me" (Ps. 42:7). Hear Him again as He cries, "Thy wrath lieth hard upon Me, and Thou hast afflicted Me with all Thy waves" (Ps. 88:7). Surely Isaac Watts was meditating on this aspect of Calvary's sufferings when he was inspired to write words that never fail to move and melt the heart of the true Christian:

> *Alas! and did my Saviour bleed?*
> *And did my Sovereign die?*
> *Would He devote that sacred head*
> *For such a worm as I?*

> *Was it for crimes that I have done*
> *He groaned upon the tree?*
> *Amazing pity! grace unknown!*
> *And love beyond degree!*

> *Well might the sun in darkness hide,*
> *And shut his glories in,*
> *When the Incarnate Maker died*
> *For man His creature's sin.*

Thus might I hide my blushing face,
While His dear Cross appears,
Dissolve my heart in thankfulness,
And melt my eyes to tears.

Indeed throughout eternity our song shall be "Unto Him that loved us, and washed us from our sins in His own blood" (Rev. 1:5).

Reviewing the situation from the time when Joseph started to deal with them until the discovery of the money in their sacks as they journeyed home, one is impressed with the fact that the men, despite all the strange happenings, seemed to be absolutely blind to the reality of the situation and that they had actually been listening to the very voice they had heard so long ago at Dothan uttering cries of anguish and distress. Why should Joseph accuse ten men together from one family as spies? Why should he hold Simeon as a hostage? Why should he be so determined that they bring Benjamin on their return? Why should the money be restored? Why should he act as he did because of the fear of God? Surely strange words for an Egyptian!

All this describes the ignorance of the natural man in relation to the things of God and His dealings with men regarding their incapability of understanding the mind and message of God as revealed in the Gospel. First Corinthians 2 verses 7-10 say, "But we speak the wisdom of God in a mystery, even the hidden wisdom, which God ordained before the world unto our glory: which none of the princes of this world knew: for had they known it, they would not have crucified the Lord of glory. But as it is written, Eye hath not seen, nor ear heard, neither have entered into the heart of man, the things which God hath prepared for them that love Him. But God hath revealed them unto us by His Spirit: for the Spirit searcheth all things, yea,

117

the deep things of God." Verse 14 goes on to say, "But the natural man receiveth not the things of the Spirit of God: for they are foolishness unto him: neither can he know them, because they are spiritually discerned."

It is easy to imagine the anxiety of the brethren as they made their way home. The thoughts of meeting their father and no Simeon with them. Too well they remembered another day when they had to face him without Joseph, carrying the blood-soaked "coat of many colors." Conscience again filled their ears with the cries of a broken-hearted father as he wailed, "It is my son's coat; an evil beast hath devoured him; Joseph is without doubt rent in pieces."

CHAPTER 22

JACOB'S DISTRESS

The brethren of Joseph must face their father again, but this time they had an explanation. But before they had time to do this no doubt the "hue and cry" would be raised, especially in the house of Simeon. When they finally told their story in full, and emphasized the fact that Simeon could not be released until they would present Benjamin to the lord of the land, Jacob was distressed and said, "Me have ye bereaved of my children: Joseph is not, and Simeon is not, and ye will take Benjamin away: all these things are against me" (42:36).

The last statement, "All these things are against me," shows the hard-pressed patriarch groaning under the weight of fresh trial. He never did get over the loss of Joseph, now he is robbed of Simeon, and as far as he can see he must part with Benjamin, the darling child of his beloved Rachel, if there was to be any hope of Simeon's release. It would seem he had allowed the trials of life to get him down, and that for the time being he had forgotten that the God of Jacob had His hand on the helm of his life. When the whole story will eventually be told, he will see that instead of "All these things are against me," every seemingly adverse happening was only furthering the Divine plan and purpose for his good and ultimate blessing.

How many of us have fallen into the same ditch as Jacob. In the day of severe trial and testing, when the sun was hidden behind the darkened clouds and we were made to feel the force of the tempest's bitter blast until at last we began to wonder if God had forgotten us. Did we then act as he did? I am afraid most of us will have to confess with shame that sometimes this has been true of us. Oh, that we might learn there are no accidents in the life of the Christian, but instead, all the happenings are incidents that are fitting into the plan and pattern God has designed! For it is certain we shall yet be made to acknowledge that:

> *The dark threads were as needful in the*
> *skilful weaver's hand,*
> *As the threads of gold and silver in the*
> *pattern God had planned.*

It is well for us to remember the words of Romans 8:28: "And we know that all things work together for good to them that love God, to them who are the called according to His purpose."

Again Reuben comes into the picture with something to say. This seems to characterize him, for he was the spokesman at Dothan; and again in the prison when he said to his brethren, "Spake I not unto you, do not sin against the child . . . ." He was a man of words but not of action. It always appeals to me that Reuben in this story is a classic illustration of the "double minded man" of whom James writes in his epistle (1:8). In Hebrew, James is really Jacob, and it is remarkable that this is the first type of man James deals with. He says, "A double minded man is UNSTABLE in all his ways," and this is the very expression that the old patriarch used when Reuben came before him in Genesis 49: "Unstable as water, thou shalt not excel."

James shows in his practical letter that the man of faith is more than a man who merely SAYS, "I have faith." "No," says James, "faith, if it hath not works, is dead, being alone. Yea, a man may say, Thou hast faith, and I have works: show me thy faith without thy works, and I will show thee my faith by my works" (2:17, 18). He then selects two outstanding characters from the Old Testament who illustrate this principle, and who stand out in contrast to the "unstable man."

First of all he considers Abraham. He believed God and showed his faith by acting promptly when God told him to offer up his son, which meant nothing short of putting him to death. We might well ask, How could he do such a thing? Had not God promised to give him an innumerable seed through Isaac? How then could this be? If he should put him to death surely all hope would be gone. To human reasoning, this was so, but Abraham believed that even should he obey God to the extent of sacrificing his beloved son and heir to the promises, yet God was able to raise him up again from the dead, "from whence also he received him in a figure" (Heb. 11:19).

Next comes Rahab. She believed the reports of Israel's invincibility, and had faith that Israel's God would conquer Jericho. So at the risk of her life, she "received the spies in peace," sent them out another way, hung the scarlet cord in the window, counting herself and family absolutely safe, and her house as still standing when Jericho's walls would fall.

Let us listen to Reuben, as old Jacob laments the loss of his sons and complains of the sore bereavement. "And Reuben spake unto his father, saying, Slay my two sons, if I bring him not to thee: deliver him into my hand, and I will bring him to thee again" (Gen. 42:37). Did he really expect his father to listen to him? Had he forgotten what was expected of him when Joseph was sent to seek the welfare of his brethren? Was he not aware that his father had

121

never forgotten his failure to protect his brother that day and bring him safely home?

On that day he had miserably failed. He was unstable, and lacked backbone to take his stand as did Joseph in the house of Potiphar. Reuben failed to act at Dothan as his child-brother's protector. Now he will not be accepted as the surety for his other child-brother, Benjamin. Poor Reuben—"Unstable as water, thou shalt not excel"! "No," said Jacob, "my son shall not go down with you; for his brother is dead, and he is left alone: if mischief befall him by the way in the which ye go, then shall ye bring down my gray hairs with sorrow to the grave" (42:38).

When you think of the number of homes that had to be supplied with food in that day of famine, it would not take long to exhaust the little store they had brought from Egypt. We read in Chapter 43:1 and 2, "And the famine was sore in the land. And it came to pass, when they had eaten up the corn which they had brought out of Egypt, their father said unto them, Go again, buy us a little food." The pressure of the famine was telling its tale, and despite Jacob's misgivings and fears for the safety of Simeon, and the risk of sending Benjamin, he was compelled to make the decision that the men should go back to Egypt. I say, he was compelled to make the decision because there was no other source of supply. The command to the seekers at the beginning was, "Go to Joseph," and this was still the only way to find a supply in the hour of need.

Jacob, being brought down to a state of dire and desperate need, would remind us of the principle that is set forth in the Gospel message. A sinner who is never made deeply aware of his need, and who does not really feel the pangs of soul hunger, will never want to seek after God's provision in Christ. It was when the prodigal spent all "and began to be in want" that his thoughts turned to the plenty of his father's home. Hear him say, "How many hired servants of my father's have bread enough and to spare, and I perish with hunger! I will arise and go to my father" (Luke 15:17, 18).

From another angle the Saviour teaches this same principle. He said, "They that be whole need not the physician, but they that are sick; I came not to call the righteous, but sinners to repentance." Is it not a lovely thought, that at the other end, the lord of the land was anxiously awaiting their return? He knew their provision, for the period they were away, must soon be at an end. Shall I say, he would be counting the days for their return, longing again to supply their outcrying need? What a picture of the Saviour! Can we not hear Him cry, "Come unto Me, all ye that labour and are heavy laden, and I will give you rest"? (Matt. 11:28). And again, "Him that cometh to Me I will in no wise cast out" (John 6:37), and yet again, "I am the Bread of life: he that cometh to Me shall never hunger" (John 6:35).

In John 5:40 we read His plaintive lament to the Jews who were self-sufficient and felt no need of Him: "Ye will not come to Me, that ye might have life." Listen to His heart-breaking wail over the holy city, outside of which He soon would be impaled on a Roman gibbet: "O Jerusalem, Jerusalem, which killest the prophets, and stonest them that are sent unto thee; how often would I have gathered thy children together, as a hen doth gather her brood under her wings, and ye would not!" (Luke 13:34).

CHAPTER 23

JUDAH – SURETY FOR BENJAMIN

Judah now comes into prominence in our story. The last time we saw him was when he exchanged the child Joseph for the price of a slave. I am sure that over the years conscience had made that money burn as it were in his very hand, and I believe he would have done anything, indeed given anything, if only he could have undone the awful deed. Here I am almost afraid to put on paper the thought that presses in upon me now.

Do you know, my mind has been carried to think of those to whom the Holy Ghost had pleaded to embrace the invitation of Christ, to come to Him for salvation and eternal life, but have turned away from Him. They have neglected Him for the pleasures of sin and love of the world. They have rejected Him, and are now, as the result of their self-willed choice, among the lost in the realm of endless despair – in the blackness of darkness forever. Oh, I ask you, what would they not do, what would they not give, if only they could get back to earth, if only they could have but one more opportunity to embrace Christ! But alas! alas! – "Too late, too late, will be the cry, Jesus of Nazareth has passed by."

If you have until now stayed away from Christ, trying, it may be, to find satisfaction in this poor, fading, transient world, I beg of you, be intreated of me, seek Him now, "while He will receive you." "The harvest is passing, the summer will end." Tomorrow could be forever too late!

In our story Judah is a picture of the sinner in *time,* and as we shall see, he was yet going to have a God-given opportunity to be reconciled to Joseph on the ground of true and manifest repentance. Here is encouragement to those who have refused the offer of salvation, not to despair, for if they will only turn to Him now, they will find His loving arms open wide to receive them.

By the time we reach Chapter 43, with the food supply running out, the situation was really becoming desperate all around. There was nothing but barren earth, languishing cattle, drying river beds, and the heavens as brass. Under the circumstances Jacob was made to see that there was no alternative but to go back to Egypt for a further supply, or sit as they were to perish and die. Judah, who now seemed to be in control of the mission, was ready to depart, but as we have noticed, when Jacob gave the command, "Go again and buy us a little food" he made no mention of Benjamin. So Judah had to remind him that the lord of the land had said, "Ye shall not see my face except your brother be with you," and added, "If thou wilt send our brother with us, we will go down and buy thee food: but if thou wilt not send him, we will not go down." One is struck with old Jacob's interjection, "Wherefore dealt ye so ill with me, as to tell the man whether ye had yet a brother?" The old twisted streak of the Jacob nature is almost seen in the forefront again. Had they kept this secret, he seemed to reason, they could have returned and yet have allowed Benjamin to remain at home. In reply to this they said, "The man asked us straitly of our state, and of our kindred, saying, Is your father yet alive? have ye another brother? and we told him according to the tenor of these words: could we certainly know that he would say, Bring your brother down?"

Verses 8-10 give us one of the most moving speeches

125

of Holy Scripture: "And Judah said unto Israel his father, Send the lad with me, and we will arise and go; that we may live, and not die, both we, and thou, and also our little ones. I will be surety for him; of my hand shalt thou require him: if I bring him not unto thee, and set him before thee, then let me bear the blame forever: for except we had lingered, surely now we had returned this second time." What a contrast to Reuben's hasty and cowardly offer, "Slay my two sons, if I bring him not to thee" (42:37)! It is no wonder Jacob said, "My son shall not go down with you." Reuben would save his own skin, even if it cost him his two loved sons. His was not the language of a true and worthy surety. Noble Judah steps in to meet the emergency. Fasten your eyes on these stirring and soul-moving words again: *"I will be surety for him, . . . if I bring him not unto thee . . . let me bear the blame for ever."* Judah meant every word of what he said, as we shall see later in the story.

This noble action of Judah directs us to Another, who, for the guilty sons of Adam's race, in a matter of life or death, stepped in to act as Surety. This aspect of the Saviour's work is indeed the very heart of the Gospel message. A surety is one who takes the responsibility for another whose credit is not good. The wise man tells us in Proverbs 11:15, "He that is surety for a stranger shall smart for it: and he that hateth suretyship is sure." The last statement here simply means, that the one who keeps clear from acting as surety, will never be held accountable for another's failure.

Consider such Scripture passages as Ezekiel 18:4, "The soul that sinneth, it shall die"; Romans 6:23, "The wages of sin is death"; Psalm 9:17, "The wicked shall be turned into hell, and all the nations that forget God"; Hebrews 9:27, "It is appointed unto men once to die, but after this the judgment." These and many more such passages cause us to realize that apart from divine intervention, and a satisfaction given to meet the claims of God's violated throne, the whole world must inevitably perish under the judgment hand of a holy and inflexibly righteous God.

When the sinner is made to face this truth, how often he turns and asks, "But is not God a God of love?" Yes, indeed, that is the very nature of His being, but His love is righteous love. Sin must be dealt with. Sin is rebellion against God and must be punished. How can this be done, and the guilty sinner escape the wrath of Almighty God? The answer can be given in one word — "CALVARY." Yes, it is there we see the Divine attributes harmonized. Psalm 85:10 puts it beautifully, "Mercy and truth are met together; righteousness and peace have kissed each other."

How often in the past I have asked my Gospel audiences to sing:

> *O wondrous love for sinners given,*
> *To save from hell, and bring to Heaven!*
> *O tell its virtues all abroad,*
> *Of love divine — the love of God.*

Yes! It was on that dark cross God's blessed Son became Surety: "There was no other good enough to pay the price of sin." Let us think of

HIS INFINITE ABILITY

It would be foolish for anyone to become surety who lacked the wherewithal to meet the demands involved. But, this is where our Surety shines. Think on who He is! The mighty Maker of the universe, the Eternal Son of the Eternal God. Yet He must die, and to die He must become a man, so we think of

HIS VOLUNTARY HUMILITY

"Great is the mystery of godliness: God was manifest in the flesh." The Word became flesh and tabernacled

127

among us (John 1:14). I direct your attention again to Philippians 2:5-8: ". . . Christ Jesus: who, being in the form of God, thought it not robbery to be equal with God: but made Himself of no reputation, and took upon Him the form of a servant, and was made in the likeness of men: and being found in fashion as a man, He humbled Himself, and became obedient unto death, even the death of the *cross.*" What words are these — "*the death of the cross*"! This would make us think of

HIS TREMENDOUS RESPONSIBILITY

On the cross "He took the guilty sinner's place and suffered in his stead." It is Blane who says —

> *Had man but one wrong action done,*
> *None but the Co-Eternal Son*
> *Could for that single sin atone,*
> *And then He must be left alone*
> *To sink beneath God's angry wave,*
> *With none to pity, none to save.*

In Isaiah 53:7, Newberry's margin expresses the Surety's responsibility in these words: "It was *exacted,* and He becometh answerable."

> *The wrath of God that was our due,*
> *Upon the Lamb was laid,*
> *And by the shedding of His blood,*
> *The debt for us was paid.*

Here the believer rests in sweetest peace and sings with deepest gratitude in his heart of Christ:

> *He bore on the tree, the sentence for me,*
> *And now both the Surety and sinner are free.*

Paul's word to the Romans comes to mind: "Who was delivered for our offences, and was raised again for our justification. Therefore being justified by faith, we

128

have peace with God through our Lord Jesus Christ" (4:25; 5:1). Now note

HIS SACRIFICIAL EFFICACY

So full and complete was the satisfaction rendered to God's violated Throne, that He fills the highest place in Heaven, and there He sits, "able . . . to save to the uttermost all that come unto God by Him."

> *Such was the sacrifice He made,*
> *The Law could ask no more,*
> *For not a mite was left unpaid,*
> *When He our judgment bore.*

We may group these precious thoughts together concerning our blessed Surety:

HIS INFINITE ABILITY — *as to His Person*

HIS VOLUNTARY HUMILITY—*as to His mighty stoop*

HIS TREMENDOUS RESPONSIBILITY—*as to His Cross*

HIS SACRIFICIAL EFFICACY—*as to cancelling the sinner's debt*

Let the Christian reader rejoice in the Surety's finished work, and, perchance, you should be still faced with the awful debt of sin, I beg you, look by faith to Calvary and claim Him as your own, and do it now.

Judah's assuring offer to safeguard Benjamin, and to return him to his father again, shows what a change of heart had come over him. Here was genuine repentance. Conscience had done its work in convincing him of the error of his ways, with the result he had his mind firmly made up never to treat a brother again as he had treated Joseph at Dothan. This decision was to prove the gateway to blessing, not only for himself, but for his old father, his brethren and all their families. Repentance is not penance, as found in the Douay Version of the Bible. Repentance is a change of mind that effects a change of course. It is a mental change

129

that works a moral change. Penance may make a man weep for his sins, but true repentance makes a man forsake the sin for which he weeps.

When Christ commissioned His disciples, repentance was linked with the forgiveness of sins. In a word, where there is no repentance there is no forgiveness. I am afraid this aspect of the Gospel is greatly neglected in these days of modern thinking. The young man in the parable who, when told by his father, "Go, work today in my vineyard," said, "I will not go," is a classic illustration of the meaning of repentance. He said, "I will not go," but afterward, "He repented and *went.*" His change of mind was proved by a change of course. Repentance is seen in—

Acts 17:30 as "The command of God"
Acts 5:31 as "The gift of Christ"
1 Thess. 1:5 as "The work of the Holy Spirit"
2 Peter 3:9 as "The desire of the Lord."

Jacob is made to see that except he complied with the conditions laid down by the lord of the land, no more food could be obtained, and Simeon must remain a prisoner in Egypt. He was made to feel the powerful tugging at his heart strings as he thought of parting with Benjamin who was, as far as he knew, the only remaining link with his departed and dearly beloved Rachel, who had died at Benjamin's birth. However, dear and much treasured as this little idol was, it had to be surrendered. It was either that or perish in the famine.

I believe there is an important Gospel lesson to be learned from the old patriarch's behavior at this time of crisis, for a time of crisis it surely was. It was a matter of life or death. As long as he was determined not to part with Benjamin, the way of blessing and deliverance was completely barred. How many a sinner, awakened to the need of salvation, and to the awful danger of perishing without it, has made no progress on the way to blessing because of the failure to part with some cherished idol that was held dearer than life! It could be a career, it could be a companion, it could be sport, it could be business. For the young ruler, it was lands and possessions. The invited guests in Luke 14 to the Great Supper were hindered by the land, the cattle and the wife. These "Benjamins" and many others, keep many souls from getting to Christ and block for them the road to Heaven. What eternal remorse will fill the lost soul, who in life allowed that cherished thing to cheat him out of God's salvation, and to cause him to miss a happy home in Heaven with Christ and all the redeemed! No wonder Jesus challenged the crowd with the gigantic question, "For what shall it profit a man, if he shall gain the whole world, and lose his own soul?" (Mark 8:36).

Let me apply this lesson to the young believers in Christ. To obtain fullness of blessing in the Christian life and service, there must be "full surrender." It has been often said, "If Christ is not Lord of *all,* He is not Lord at all." Anything that would draw away the affections of the heart from Christ is an idol. There are many temptations in the young believer's path. It may be the ambition to get on in life, and to achieve success. Earthly and material things may fill up all of one's time, with the result that the things of God have to take the second place, and the road to the "fulness of blessing" is barred. How often I have stood back and admired Paul the apostle when he said, "According to my earnest expectation and my hope, that in nothing I shall be ashamed, but that with all boldness, as always, so now also Christ shall be magnified in my body, whether it be by life, or by death" (Phil. 1:20). And again when he said, "For me to live is *Christ.*" It is well for young and old alike to give heed to the Saviour's word in Matthew 6:33, "But seek ye

131

first the kingdom of God, and His righteousness; and all these things shall be added unto you." How one should covet Frances R. Havergal's condition of soul when she wrote:

> *Take my life and let it be*
> *Consecrated, Lord, to Thee;*
> *Take my moments and my days,*
> *Let them flow in ceaseless praise.*

> *Take my will and make it Thine,*
> *It shall be no longer mine;*
> *Take my heart, it is Thine own;*
> *It shall be Thy royal throne.*

When we reach to these heights, "the things of earth grow strangely dim" and Christ becomes all, and in all.

The introduction of Benjamin into the picture suggests another very precious line of teaching relative to the Gospel. When he was born, his dying mother Rachel called him *Benoni,* that means "The son of my sorrow." But Jacob protested that he should be called *Benjamin,* which means "The son of the right hand." When you think of these joint names, of whom are you reminded? For me, I think at once of the once *humiliated* but now exalted Saviour. The first title reminds us of "The Man of Sorrows," as He was when here on earth; the second title points us up to "The Son on the right hand of the Throne." Looking at Benjamin in this typical way, and remembering that the lord of the land said, "Ye shall not see my face, except your brother be with you," reminds us in the Gospel sense that no sinner will ever know divine acceptance, or obtain the necessary provision to meet his soul's deep need, apart from bringing Christ to God as his only plea. Right on the threshold of the Bible we are told Abel was accepted by God because he brought his lamb, speaking of Christ, "The Lamb of God." Cain was rejected because he failed to do so;

132

instead, he brought that which was merely the work of his own hands.

In Bunyan's famous allegory, *Pilgrim's Progress,* Ignorance reaches the door of the Celestial City, but when asked from whence he had come and what he would have, he answered, "I have eaten and drunk in the presence of the King, and He has taught in our streets." Then they asked him for his certificate, that they might go in and show it to the King; so he fumbled in his bosom for one and found none. Then, adds Bunyan, "I saw there was a way to Hell, even from the very gates of Heaven." Dear reader, be sure you have Christ and His finished work as your certificate, for only then will your entrance to the Eternal City, be fully assured.

133

CHAPTER 24

JUDAH'S URGENT PLEA

Now turn back to Judah's convincing argument for a return to Egypt. Not only did he pledge himself to be surety for Benjamin, but he added, "For except we had lingered, surely now we had returned this second time." What a dangerous position they had put themselves into by lingering! The supply they had already brought was melting away, and how were they to know but the lord of the land had worked out an approximate time for their return. Did it not strike old Jacob that the longer he held Benjamin, the longer poor Simeon must languish in prison? How long they were overdue can be seen from Judah's words, for he said had they not lingered, "surely now we had returned this second time." They actually could have been to Egypt and back. Where was the patriarch's faith now?

We are made to see that the best of men are only failing men at best! But for Jacob's undue favoritism, which is most undesirable in any family, he could have been sitting in the good of a second bountiful supply, with Simeon and Benjamin at his side. Had he not a God who styled Himself "The God of Jacob"? Was He not the God who had worked for him and intervened on his behalf all along the way? From this lingering attitude surely there is something that we might learn. It would seem to say, "Beware of needless and unwise delays."

To put off a pressing duty till tomorrow, to hesitate when we ought to resolve, is dangerous and could prove fatal. What a golden opportunity Felix had to embrace salvation on that day when the great Paul reasoned with him, but alas, he put it off to a more convenient season. In a word, he said, "Tomorrow," but that tomorrow never came. Thousands of souls have missed salvation by falling into the same snare. The only other time the word "lingered" is used in the Old Testament is Genesis 19:16 when Lot was leaving Sodom, before the fire and brimstone fell. It says, "While he *lingered,* the men laid hold upon his hand, and upon the hand of his wife, and upon the hand of his two daughters." Was it because they were loath to leave and break with all their former associates? As far as Lot's wife was concerned no doubt that was the reason. Despite the fact that she was told not to look back, the pull of Sodom was too great, for that is just exactly what she did, and perished as the result. She was lost though she had been put on the way to safety by an angel hand. The very morning Caesar was murdered he had a letter put into his hand by Artemidorus telling him of the plot, but he was so busy he neglected to open it. Had he but spared a moment to open the letter, instead of putting it off, he could have saved his life. Well said the wise man, "Boast not thyself of tomorrow; for thou knowest not what a day may bring forth" (Prov. 27:1).

> *"Tomorrow," he promised his conscience,*
> *"Tomorrow I mean to believe,*
> *Tomorrow I'll think as I ought to,*
> *Tomorrow my Saviour receive,*
> *Tomorrow I'll conquer the habits*
> *That hold me from Heaven away."*
> *But ever God's Spirit made answer—*
> *One word and one only—"Today."*
> *Tomorrow, Tomorrow, Tomorrow,*
> *Thus day after day it went on;*
> *Tomorrow, Tomorrow, Tomorrow,*
> *Till youth, like a vision, had gone,*
> *Till age, and his passion had written*
> *The message, "Too late!" on his brow,*
> *And forth from the shadows came death*
> *With its pitiless syllable — NOW!*

135

CHAPTER 25

BENJAMIN GOES TO EGYPT

It would seem that Judah's earnest appeal brought Jacob to his senses. He saw the folly of his partial dealings and his inexcusable behavior in holding back the blessing of God in a day of outcrying and desperate need. The plight that Simeon was in also was beginning to register as well, with the result faith triumphs, and rises to action. "And their father Israel [note the name — not "Jacob"] said unto them, If it must be so now, do this; take of the best fruits in the land in your vessels, and carry down the man a present, a little balm, and a little honey, spices, and myrrh, nuts, and almonds: and take double money in your hand; and the money that was brought again in the mouth of your sacks, . . . peradventure it was an oversight: take also your brother, and arise, go again unto the man: and GOD ALMIGHTY give you mercy before the man, that he may send away your other brother, and Benjamin. If I be bereaved of my children, I am bereaved" (Gen. 43:11-14).

The fact that Jacob is spoken of as *Israel,* his princely and prevailing name, brings him to the forefront again as "the man of faith." He is prepared to launch out into the unknown, relying upon Jehovah. As he spoke the word of command to the men, "Go again unto the man" he had no idea what would be the outcome. They had been treated so roughly on their first visit — three days in prison, accused of being spies, Simeon kept as an hostage until Benjamin would be produced, and then what seemed so contradictory, their money returned and found in their sack's mouth.

Faith has been described as "Trusting God in the dark." It is instructive to go back and remember the critical circumstances in which Jacob was found when God changed his name. In Chapter 32:24, having sent his company over the brook Jabbok, we read, "And Jacob was left alone; and there wrestled a man with him until the breaking of the day." It was no less a person than the Angel of Jehovah. At the breaking of the day, the man said to Jacob, "Let me go, for the day breaketh." Jacob replied, "I will not let thee go, except thou bless me." And the man said unto him, "What is thy name?" And he said, "Jacob." And he said, "Thy name shall be called no more Jacob, but *Israel*: for as a prince hast thou power with God and with men, and hast prevailed." And Jacob called the name of the place "Peniel: for I have seen God face to face, and my life is preserved."

This memorable event took place as Esau was advancing to meet him with four hundred men. The odds were very much against Jacob and enough to cause the stoutest heart to fear, yet he moved forward to meet his offended brother, only to find that all his fears were groundless, for Esau ran to meet him, and fell on his neck, and kissed him. Already the meaning of his new name had been displayed, for he had been received as a prince, and with men he had prevailed.

This is the spirit in which we now find Jacob in our story as he sends the men off to Egypt. Jacob is now "the man of faith" and "the liberal man," for he would send with them a valuable present consisting of the best fruits of the land, for despite the fact of their lack

137

of corn, they had some precious commodities which were not to be found in Egypt, or at least not to be found there in such perfection. It was not by any means a great and rich present such as would be offered to a lord in Egypt's land, but it was the best of its kind. The impression he got of the rough-speaking lord would make one think he would have little notion of sending him a present. Had he in his mind how well the present worked when he was going out to meet Esau, the one whose birthright he had taken? He also told them to take double money in their hand, saying, "Peradventure it was an oversight." It was to be expected that double money would be needed, not only to prove as they said, that they were true men, by returning the money that was in their sacks, but also because the price of corn was bound to soar as the famine persisted. In this Jacob showed himself as "the man of integrity." He would take no advantage of the oversight of those with whom he dealt. As one has said, "No man of integrity will take an unrighteous advantage to himself of the mistakes of his neighbour." So the first money had to be restored because, "Peradventure it was an oversight," and now his last word to them as "the dependent man," "And *God Almighty* give you mercy before the man."

He falls back with his burden on EL SHADDAI — the *All-sufficient God* leaning on His *mercy*. The command given and the instructions completed, we have his touching appendix, "If I be bereaved of my children, I am bereaved." Underneath these words we may read his willing submission to the will of the Covenant-keeping God. True, he had mourned long and sore for Joseph, Simeon was lying in an Egyptian prison, and now the child Benjamin must be separated from him not knowing what would befall him. It would seem he had wakened up to the fact that such a situation could not have arisen apart from all these trials having a place in the divine purpose. To sum up Jacob's conduct at this crisis we see him as:

> *The man of faith;*
> *The man of beneficence;*
> *The man of integrity;*
> *The man of dependence;*
> *The man of resignation.*

It is well for God's children, when things seem to be going against them and heavy trials cross their pathway, to remember Isaiah 26:3, 4: "Thou wilt keep him in perfect peace, whose mind is stayed on Thee: because he trusteth in Thee. Trust ye in the LORD for ever: for in the LORD JEHOVAH is everlasting strength [marg. the Rock of Ages]." Also James 1:12, "Blessed is the man that endureth temptation [trial]: for when he is tried, he shall receive the crown of life, which the Lord hath promised to them that love Him." The resigned Christian can sing,

> *Every trial draws Him nearer;*
> *Peace, peace is mine.*

CHAPTER 26

THE SECOND VISIT TO EGYPT

The brethren now take Benjamin with them and set out the second time to buy corn in Egypt. It was with more anxiety of heart, than Joseph ever knew on his way to the slave market in Egypt. The readiness of Benjamin to accompany them would show that he knew nothing of how they had treated his brother Joseph. All he knew was that Joseph was dead. Certainly their sin had been concealed for a long time. However, they were soon to learn that although sin's track had been so long covered, the day of reckoning had to be faced, bringing with it a full exposure in merciless detail. This principle is illustrated in an Old Testament story in Joshua 7.

When Jericho was captured by Israel, all the spoil was consecrated unto the Lord, and a curse was placed upon anyone who dared touch it. A man called Achan saw a goodly Babylonish garment, two hundred shekels of silver and a wedge of gold. These he coveted, took them and buried them in his tent. Who was to know? He had forgotten the words of a woman who in an earlier day said, "Thou God seest me" (Gen. 16:13). Because of his high-handed act, Israel suffered an inglorious defeat. Joshua was told by God that Israel had sinned in the accursed thing, and he instructed him to call out the twelve tribes. From the tribes, Judah was taken; from the tribe of Judah, the family of the Zarhites was taken; next came the family of Zabdi; and finally Achan was taken. His sin now brought to light, he, and all that he had, died under the curse of

God in the valley of Achor. This illustration under-
lines the truth of Numbers 32:23: "Be sure your sin
will find you out." Before the second visit to Egypt
was over, Joseph's brethren were to find out this truth
in their own case.

Evidently there was nothing eventful on the journey.
We are not even told how it appealed to the lad Benjamin, although it must have been a wonderful experience for him who had never been far from home. No
doubt he would have many questions to ask. Knowing how the others had been treated on the last occasion, and the lord-of-the-land's desire to see him,
would doubtlessly cause him to wonder how he himself would fare. It was surely going to be an ordeal
for a shepherd lad to face the governor of the land.
By this time he was fully aware that apart from his
going, there would be no release for Simeon, and no
more corn for Hebron.

When they arrived in Egypt the brethren were ushered into the presence of Joseph, who was still unknown to them. They were ready to give the lord of
the land their father's present, but no notice of this
was taken by Joseph. Indeed, there was no mention
made of it whatever, for when he "saw Benjamin with
them, he said to the ruler of his house, Bring these
men home, and slay, and make ready; for these men
shall dine with me at noon" (Gen. 43:16). Judging
by the dates of the Newberry Bible, Benjamin would
be a lad of about sixteen. As we have said, it surely
was an ordeal for him to be in such strange surround-
ings. The steward brought them into Joseph's house;
this made them more afraid, and they said, "Because
of the money that was returned in our sacks at the
first time are we brought in; that he may seek occasion
against us, and fall upon us, and take us for bondmen, and our asses" (Gen. 43:18).

Before going in they made known their fears to the

141

steward. They said, "O sir, we came indeed down at the first time to buy food: and it came to pass, when we came to the inn, that we opened our sacks, and, behold, every man's money was in the mouth of his sack, our money in full weight: and we have brought it again in our hand. And other money have we brought down in our hands to buy food: we cannot tell who put our money in our sacks." And he said unto them, "Peace be to you, fear not: your God, and the God of your father, hath given you treasure in your sacks" (Gen. 43:20-23).

Judging by the brethren's spirited oration to the steward they were filled with fear and evil forebodings. Conscience was still hammering at them for continuing to cover up their sin and deception, causing them to look at every happening, as an evidence of divine displeasure. Was this going to be a secret session, demanding a reason for their delay in returning? It certainly was a great relief to them when the steward cleared up the mystery of the money in their sacks. The next act of the steward lightened their burden still further for we read, "He brought Simeon out unto them. And . . . brought the men into Joseph's house, and gave them water, and they washed their feet; and he gave their asses provender [fodder]" (43:23, 24).

Would it not seem strange to them to hear an Egyptian use such language as "your God and the God of your father." Surely that was a Hebrew expression. This should have made them think, and ask themselves, "Where did he learn that?" How blind they were to the reality of the situation, and the working out of the plan that was so soon to expose their long-hidden guilty past!

Behind the scenes, the great noonday feast was being prepared, but a word first about the part played by Joseph's steward, the ruler of his house, or house manager, for that really is the meaning of the word steward. In the New Testament the Christian is looked upon as a steward, this implying his responsibility in the honored place that he fills as the Lord's servant. A steward is one who is put in trust with his master's goods, to use and distribute, not as owner but as servant, in view of a day when he must render the account. To look at the Christian's life from this angle, gives rise for a real exercise of heart, and is bound to have a most sobering effect.

In 1 Peter 4:10, the Christian is called a steward "of the manifold grace of God." The word "manifold" touches every aspect of Christian life and service, no matter how high or how menial the service. Peter says, "As every man hath received the gift, even so minister . . ." This does not just mean teaching or preaching. It embraces whatever gift the Lord has given, for there has been entrusted to every Christian a something for the use of which he is responsible, and for which he must give account to his Lord in that coming day. In Luke 16, the Lord, in a parable, holds out a solemn warning to the Christian steward. He tells of a steward called before his master to give account of his service, for he had been wasting his master's goods. Unable to make any defense for his unfaithfulness, he is expelled from his master's service with these words, "Thou mayest be no longer steward." For this to happen in a Christian's life would be a great tragedy. The matter of eternal security does not arise here, but rather one's opportunity of service being terminated, because of unfaithfulness with that which the Lord had committed to be held in trust for Him, and used for His glory. The following words are thought-provoking.

> *When the great Eternal Auditor,*
> *My book of life reviews,*
> *And He checks my daily entries*
> *That are written on the leaves,*

143

May He find them then in order,
And no need for fear or shame,
But a balance carried forward,
To the glory of His name.

Paul in 1 Corinthians 9:27 dreaded the experience of the unfaithful steward: He tells how he put himself under the most strict discipline, "lest that by any means, when I have preached to others, I myself should be a castaway [or disapproved]." If, reader, you are interested to trace the New Testament teaching on this important subject I suggest you look at the five aspects of stewardship as given in the following outline:

Stewards of the manifold grace of God — the honor for every Christian (1 Peter 4:10)

Stewards of the people of God — the overseer in the church (Titus 1:7)

Stewards of the mysteries of God — the teacher and expositor (1 Cor. 4:2)

Stewards of the Gospel of God — the Gospel preacher (1 Cor. 9:17)

Stewards of the provision of God—the servant in the house (Luke 12:42)

Now back to the story to think of the many things that would rush into the mind and memory of Joseph. While still ignoring the present, his hungry eyes feasted on Benjamin. The last time he saw him he was but a year old. This would recall his mother Rachel's death which took place when Benjamin was born, and make him feel again the crushing blow received by Jacob his father, when so shortly after the loss of his beloved Rachel, the blood-stained "coat of many colors" stared him in the face, plunging him into years of mourning and unutterable grief. It is quite possible that as Joseph studied the face of Benjamin, he would trace in it the features of their loved mother, whose love and care he had known in Hebron until he was sixteen years of age. All these memories crowding in upon him were beginning to overpower him.

CHAPTER 27

THE GREAT NOONDAY FEAST

With a busy morning of preparation now at an end, the time arrived for the noonday feast, when the eleven brethren would dine with the lord of the land, and the Egyptian elite. On the stroke of the hour, Joseph, the lord of the land, stepped into the great hall, where the assembled guests were awaiting him. Look at the brethren as they bow themselves to the earth! Immediately he puts the question to them, "Is your father well, the old man of whom ye spake? Is he yet alive?" And they answered, "Thy servant our father is in good health, he is yet alive." And they bowed down their heads and made obeisance (Gen. 43:27, 28).

Surely here is the fulfillment of the second dream, which Joseph dreamed away back yonder in Hebron's vale. Not only are the eleven stars making obeisance to his star, but also Jacob, being presented to him as his *servant,* and his heart being still one with his departed Rachel, would answer to the sun and the moon, likewise doing obeisance.

Again Joseph fixes his eyes on Benjamin, his mother's son, and asks, "Is this your younger brother, of whom ye spake unto me? And he said, God be gracious unto thee, my son" (Gen. 43:29). By this time Joseph was again at breaking point. Without explanation he took his exit, and hastened to his own private chamber where he could weep, for his heart was deeply moved for his brother (v. 30). His feelings relieved,

145

and all traces of his grief removed, he returns as lord of the land to the feast in the banquet hall.

Retaining the dignity consistent with his elevated position, he sits down by himself in the place of honor. Near to him sat the brethren by themselves, then the Egyptian guests by themselves. The placing of the brethren at the table is another episode in the working out of Joseph's plan. They sat before him, the first-born according to his birthright, and the youngest according to his youth, so that the men marveled one at another. Did it not strike them that there was someone in the company who knew all about them, one who knew them so well as to put them in their proper place? It simply says, "The men marveled one at another." Joseph himself then sent them their portions, and Benjamin's portion was five times more than any of theirs. Of course this was the custom in those days. The outstanding guest got the special portion. It was evident that the brethren in no way showed themselves envious of their youngest brother.

Yet how is it that they did not ask themselves again why Benjamin should be shown this special favor? In what sense was he to be more favored by the lord of the land than they? If they could only have seen Joseph a little while before in his private chamber sobbing his heart out, then they would have known the reason. Link by link the chain was forming that would drag these men out into the open, bringing to light their foul deed which had been kept hidden these many years. Yet despite all the strange happenings, they still try to keep it dark. Looking at Joseph's unique position at the feast, sitting there in all his solitary dignity, we turn again to the great antitype. Romans 8:29 points onward to the coming glory, when the Christian shall sit with Christ in realms above. On that day He is seen filling the "first place" as the "Firstborn among many brethren." Colossians 1:18

says, "And He is the head of the body, the church: . . . the firstborn from the dead; that in *all* things He might have the preeminence." Yes, Christ the First-born shall stand alone, in that unique place of un-paralleled glory, far above all.

> *Far above all, far above all,*
> *God hath exalted Him far above all,*
> *Thrones and dominions before Him shall fall,*
> *Jesus, the Saviour, is far above all.*

Joseph, perceiving the attitude of the brethren toward Benjamin, who was treated as the distinguished guest, quickly detected a change of heart in them. How differently he himself had been treated, because of the favor his father had bestowed upon him, giving him the "coat of many colors." This was why they had treated him so ill; also because of the dreams he had they hated him yet the more. How different now was their treatment of Benjamin. Would the way he received Benjamin not have made them think, for surely when he said, "God be gracious to thee, my son," he spoke the language of Canaan!

We are not told of the conversation that passed between Joseph and his brethren while the feast lasted, but we can be sure Joseph got no end of information about the vale of Hebron, and about the father and his patriarchal ancestry, of which they were all so proud. Would they tell of the death of Benjamin's mother, and the tragic circumstances that attended it? Of course, they would be sure not to tell that Benjamin had a brother who was about sixteen when she passed away. That was the skeleton in the closet. They had already told the lord of Egypt, when speaking about the family, that "one is not." That was all they dared to tell.

Merry and pleasing as the noonday feast had been, like every other pleasure, it was soon to pass. For the

147

time being they had forgotten the black inky past. But the voice of conscience could not be silenced, as it continually cried, "God requireth that which is past" (Eccles. 3:15). Let me speak a word to the pleasure lover. The Bible tells us that the pleasures of sin are only for a season. They are short-lived. The great danger is, when one gets obsessed and absorbed with the pleasures of this life, thoughts of God and eternity are ruled out. The story is told of the king who asked a craftsman to make him something that resembled the pleasures of life. He set to work and produced a beautiful bowl, filled it with luscious wine, and gave it to his majesty to drink. He drank deeply, but as he came near the dregs, he saw a coiled-up serpent with its fangs ready to strike. "I see," said the king, "the pleasures of life are sweet at the time, but at the end they have a sting." How true, in the case of so many, is the old hymn:

> *Room for pleasure, room for business,*
> *But for Christ the crucified,*
> *Not a place that He can enter,*
> *In the heart for which He died.*

For the Christian, life is full of pleasure now, and as to the future, the Psalmist says, "In Thy presence is fulness of joy; at Thy right hand there are pleasures for evermore" (Ps. 16:11).

CHAPTER 28

THE HOMEWARD JOURNEY BEGINS

With the night of feasting over, Joseph "commanded the steward of his house, saying, 'Fill the men's sacks with food, as much as they can carry, and put every man's money in his sack's mouth. And put my cup, the silver cup, in the sack's mouth of the youngest, and his corn money.' And he did according to the word that Joseph had spoken. As soon as the morning was light, the men were sent away, they and their asses. And when they were gone out of the city, and not yet far off, Joseph said unto his steward, 'Up, follow after the men; and when thou dost overtake them, say unto them, Wherefore have ye rewarded evil for good? Is not this it in which my lord drinketh, and whereby indeed he divineth? ye have done evil in so doing' " (Gen. 44:1-5).

One can see the thoughtfulness of Joseph, in sending them away as soon as the morning was light; this saved them the embarrassment of Egyptian prying eyes; the fact that he let them go only a very short distance before they were made to return made it possible for them to be back before Egypt was really awake. Joseph had no desire to make them a gazing-stock. If his guilty brethren were to have their sin exposed, it would be in his own presence, and not before the world. Is not this God's way with the repentant sinner still? To be sure, it is! Has sin to be confessed and guilt to be acknowledged? Then to whom will the sin-

149

ner go? Must the matter be blazened abroad? Bless
God, no! Think of Charlotte Elliott's words:

> *Just as I am, and waiting not*
> *To rid my soul of one dark blot;*
> *To Thee, whose blood can cleanse each spot,*
> *O Lamb of God, I come.*

In the New Testament it was the father to whom
the prodigal returned, and to him alone he made confession. How kindly and feelingly Joseph dealt with
his brethren. No doubt they set out on their journey
that early morning in cheerful spirits. They had another supply of corn for their father and their little
ones. They had met with great kindness from the lord
of Egypt, who on their first visit seemed to treat them
with such undeserved harshness. Simeon and Benjamin were with them. It would be only a few days
until they would arrive at Hebron, bringing cheer to
their old father, and the waiting families.

Alas, this beautiful morning for them was soon to
be overcast with dark clouds. They had not gone very
far when they heard a rider coming with speed to overtake them, and who was it but the steward! It was
the very one who only a short time before, had filled
their sacks and sent them on their way! On reaching
them he dismounted quickly and immediately leveled
a very serious charge against them in these words,
"Wherefore have ye rewarded evil for good? Is not
this it in which my lord drinketh? and whereby indeed
he divineth? ye have done evil in so doing." Loudly
they protested saying, " 'Wherefore saith my lord these
words? God forbid that thy servants should do according to this thing: Behold, the money, which we
found in our sacks' mouths, we brought again unto
thee out of the land of Canaan: how then should we
steal out of thy lord's house silver or gold? With whom-

soever of thy servants it be found, both let him die, and we also will be my lord's bondmen.' And he said, 'Now also let it be according unto your words: he with whom it is found shall be my servant; and ye shall be blameless.' Then they speedily took down every man his sack to the ground, and opened every man his sack. And he searched, and began at the eldest, and left at the youngest: and the cup was found in Benjamin's sack. Then they rent their clothes, and laded every man his ass, and returned to the city" (Gen. 44:5-13).

What an abrupt ending to their cheerful homegoing! How could we but feel sorry for Benjamin? Well he knew that, although the cup was found in his sack, it was not of his doing. But how could he clear himself? Circumstantial evidence was all against him, so there was nothing left for the company to do, but to return and face the governor. This telling part of Joseph's plan was merely enacted to hurry them back, for his heart was breaking. Well he knew by this happening he would have convincing proof that his brethren had indeed undergone a change of heart. If they were prepared to stand by the lad, despite the fact that he was the cause for their return, what a change this would be from the day they tore from him his "coat of many colors," threw him into a pit, and then sold him into a life of slavery, and deceived the old father, plunging him into a life of sorrow and mourning.

What a beautiful foreshadowing of the Lord Jesus Christ we have here. Peter says of Him, "When He was reviled, reviled not again; when He suffered, He threatened not" (1 Peter 2:23). It was on Calvary there came from the suffering Saviour's lips these immortal words, "Father, forgive them; for they know not what they do" (Luke 23:34). Peter tells the Christian that Christ has left us an example that we should follow His steps (1 Peter 2:21). What is more to be

151

coveted in the life of a Christian, than a forgiving spirit!

One day Peter asked the Lord, "How oft shall my brother sin against me, and I forgive him? till seven times?" Jesus said unto him, "I say not unto thee, Until seven times: but, Until seventy times seven" (Matt. 18:21, 22). Then comes the story of the man who owed his master ten thousand talents, but because he had nothing to meet the debt and pleaded for mercy, the master had compassion on him and freely forgave him. The servant now freely forgiven, found one of his fellow-servants who owed him one hundred pennies and he took him by the throat, saying, "Pay me that thou owest." And his fellow-servant fell down at his feet, and besought him, saying, "Have patience with me and I will pay thee all." These are the words he himself had used when he got his master's forgiveness, but he would not forgive, but cast the poor debtor into prison, till he should pay the debt. News reached the generous forgiving master's ears, so he summoned the forgiven debtor to appear before him, and when he did, he charged him with his cruel treatment of his fellow servant. The result was his lord was wroth, and delivered him to the tormentors, till he should pay all that was due to him. Then Jesus adds these words, "So likewise shall My heavenly Father do also unto you, if ye from your hearts forgive not every one his brother their trespasses" (Matt. 18:35). Just here in my wide-margin Bible I penned the following lines:

> *Forgiven: and since from my Lord*
> *So oft I've heard it, and so free,*
> *Shall I refuse to speak the word*
> *To one who has offended me?*
> *No love divine can ever live*
> *Within a heart that can't forgive.*

Forgiven: this sweet word begets
The Master's spirit in the heart,
Which others' faults forgive, forgets,
And lives but blessing to impart.
He little knows of God or Heaven,
Who holds another unforgiven.

Before we return with the brethren to Joseph's house, I would like to say a word to the young reader who may be shaping into life in the big world. Let us not forget it has many snares and traps for youthful feet. The wise man of the Old Testament calls to you, "Remember now thy Creator in the days of thy youth" (Eccles. 12:1). Joseph would not let the brethren go "very far off" before they were arrested, for he had in his heart to forgive them and bless them. This book may fall into the hands of some who have heard the call of God to repent and believe the Gospel, before they would move into an alluring and deceitful world with its many paths that lead to eternal ruin and misery. Hear the words of the Saviour, "For what shall it profit a man, if he shall gain the whole world, and lose his own soul?" (Mark 8:36). How many there are who in early days did hear the call of God, to embrace Christ as Saviour, and become the possessor of eternal life, but refused to listen, or, it may be, postponed the matter. With what result? Never again were they brought to the same point of concern about eternal realities, even though they lived on for many years. To decide for Christ when one is young, means a life saved, and affords the possibility of devoting the remaining years to the honored service of God.

Catherine Booth, so-called mother of the Salvation Army, received Christ as Saviour at six-and-a-half years; Jonathan Edwards at seven, Richard Baxter at eight, Isaac Watts at nine, Graham Scroggie at nine-and-a-half, Matthew Henry at ten, C. H. Spurgeon at

twelve, General Booth at twelve, General Gordon
twelve, just to mention a few. One would say th
great servants of God were not allowed to get "u
far off" until they were arrested, brought to confess
of their sins, and received the blessing of sins forgi
and the gift of eternal life.

CHAPTER 29

RETRACING THEIR STEPS

We will now let our thoughts travel with these shocked and confused men as they make their way back to meet the lord of the land. Their out going had been bright and cheerful with the happy prospect of a welcome home by those who anxiously awaited their return. Now all is changed, and every step is filled with evil forebodings. It was bad enough the first time to be dealt with as spies, but this is far worse. Now they must stand before the governor, accused of theft, and what could they say for themselves, for there lay the evidence in the mouth of Benjamin's sack! Little did they know Joseph's design in all this. The manner in which they treated the lad would indicate whether or not they had received the change of heart he so much desired to find. On the way back, would they upbraid Benjamin? Would they decide to let him face the charge, and, if needs be, become a slave in Egypt?

Joseph was well aware what the thought of slavery in Egypt for the lad would produce in these men. Once they actually sold him to slavery, without a cause, and well he knew the lashing of conscience these men must have had over the years, not only for the wrong they had done him, but for the unutterable grief they had caused their old father. No doubt on the way back, the "coat of many colors," soaked with blood, was again confronting them. Did they hear again his heart-rending cries at Dothan, as they handed him over to the merchantmen for twenty pieces of silver? Again, what a problem they had to face, should they have to return without Benjamin! They saw what it cost their old father when they laid before him the blood-stained coat. In fact to return without Benjamin they knew would mean the death of the broken-hearted patriarch. What a dilemma they were in!

Genesis 44:14 says, "And Judah and his brethren came to Joseph's house; *for he was yet there:* and they fell before him on the ground." The words "He was yet there," have a story to tell. It was impossible for Joseph to rest; he had already seen the kindly attitude toward Benjamin expressed by the brethren, and was fully persuaded in his mind that they would soon return and take their stand in defense of the lad. Hence Joseph's waiting attitude, waiting to receive them, longing to make himself known to them, to speak to them the word of forgiveness, and place upon their cheek the kiss of reconciliation. What a picture is this of the Lord Jesus Christ, the Saviour of sinners, as He waits with outstretched arms to receive the returning sinner. Listen to His beautiful invitation, "Come unto Me, all ye that labour, and are heavy laden, and I will give you rest" (Matt. 11:28).

A woman who heard Him say these great words as she stood in the crowd was so gripped by them, that she followed Jesus into a house where He was being entertained. Being a sinner burdened with guilt, she knew what the Saviour's words "heavy laden" meant, and she embraced the invitation when the Saviour said, "Come unto Me . . . and I will give you rest." She felt this word was just for her. Having gotten into the house, see her crouch at His feet, pour upon them those scalding tears of repentance, and then tenderly wipe them with her long flowing tresses. Having brought an alabaster box of ointment with her, she also anointed the Saviour's feet. The host, seeing her do so, demurred, saying, "This man, if He were a prophet, would have known who and what manner of woman this is that toucheth Him: for she is a sinner" (Luke 7:39). But the Saviour rebuked him by the use of that meaningful parable that follows. As He turned to the broken, confessing sinner, knowing full well the weight of her burden, and commending her for taking Him at His word, He said to the host, "I say unto thee, Her sins, which are many, are forgiven; for she loved much: but to whom little is forgiven, the same loveth little." Then looking on the woman He said unto her, "Thy sins are forgiven. . . . Thy faith hath saved thee; go in peace" (Luke 7:47-50).

Joseph "was yet there" waiting to speak the word of forgiveness, waiting to lift the burden. The removal of all sense of distance would surely foreshadow the loving, gracious Saviour, who in like manner waits, as we have said, with deepest longing to welcome the returning sinner.

As these confused and broken men made their way back, you notice how Judah took the lead, for it says, "Judah and his brethren came to Joseph's house." It is evident by this time that Judah had acquired great respect among his brethren. Judah is foremost, not Reuben, though he was the oldest of the family and naturally would have been expected to take the leading role, especially in the present circumstances. No, it was Judah, and by his masterly handling of the situation, evinces something of that regal dignity that was to mark the royal tribe of which he was the father. In this connection I am made to think of the New Testament word, "It is evident that our Lord sprang out of Judah" (Heb. 7:14). There it is the question of His Royal Priesthood, the One who ever liveth to make intercession for His people. We are about to see how Judah in this very respect is again a type of our exalted Lord Jesus Christ in His present session at

157

the right hand of God, who also maketh intercession for us.

As they entered the presence of the lord of the land, we read, "And they fell before him on the ground." They could go no lower. The steward's word from Joseph was, "He with whom the cup is found, shall be my servant; and ye shall be blameless." Why not let Benjamin plead his own cause, and clear himself, if he could, of the serious charge laid against him? Why should all the others assume responsibility? It was not in any of their sacks that the cup was found. Little did they know Joseph's master plan, for in every step they took, they were fitting in the part that was about to complete it, and produce the desired effect for which Joseph was eagerly waiting. The lord of the land is the first to speak. And he said unto them, "What deed is this that ye have done? wot ye not that such a man as I can certainly divine" (or make trial)?

CHAPTER 30

JUDAH THE ADVOCATE

Now Judah, the spokesman for the rest, makes an-swer: "What shall we say unto my lord? what shall we speak? or how shall we clear ourselves? God hath found out the iniquity of thy servants: behold, we are my lord's servants, both we, and he also with whom the cup is found" (Gen. 44:16). Note: *"we . . . also."* They link themselves with Benjamin. How this act pierced the heart of Joseph, but yet he would probe even deeper! He replied in these words, "God forbid that I should do so: but the man in whose hand the cup is found, he shall be my servant; and as for you, get you up in peace unto your father." The acid test was now applied. This was Joseph's final probe. It produced the desired result as we shall immediately see. The words of Joseph "Get you up in peace unto your father" are significant. This suggestion was made to test them. It gave Joseph pleasure to find that it was not accepted. Verse 18 says, "Then Judah came near unto him, and said, Oh my lord, let thy servant, I pray thee, speak a word in my lord's ears, and let not thine anger burn against thy servant: for thou art even as Pharaoh." There is no record of Judah ever having attended the schools of advanced learning, and yet no orator ever engaged in a more powerful and moving oration. His deep conviction of Benjamin's innocency, and his affection for his venerable father, coupled with the fact that he became surety for the lad, taught him the eloquence needed for the occasion.

159

No counselor, be he ever so clever and weighty in his arguments, could equal the extempore speech of noble Judah, every word of it falling like a heavy hammer blow on the already breaking heart of Joseph. It was by no means long, and contained no unnecessary filling in. Time it for yourself as you read it, and you will find its duration is two minutes. Such pleading in language so tender, graphic and earnest, could not fail to win the day, and win the day it did.

Let us consider it just as the Scripture gives it from verse 18 to 34:

Then Judah came near unto [the governor] and said, Oh my lord, let thy servant, I pray thee, speak a word in my lord's ears, and let not thine anger burn against thy servant: for thou art even as Pharaoh. My lord asked his servants, saying, Have ye a father or a brother? And we said unto my lord, We have a father, an old man, and a child of his old age, a little one; and his brother is dead, and he alone is left of his mother, and his father loveth him. And thou saidst unto thy servants, Bring him down unto me, that I may set mine eyes upon him. And we said unto my lord, The lad cannot leave his father: for if he should leave his father, his father would die. And thou saidst unto thy servants, Except your youngest brother come down with you, ye shall see my face no more. And it came to pass when we came up unto thy servant my father, we told him the words of my lord. And our father said, Go again, and buy us a little food. And we said, We cannot go down: if our youngest brother be with us, then will we go down: for we may not see the man's face, except our youngest brother be with us. And thy servant my father said unto us, Ye know that my wife bare me two sons: and the one went out from me, and I said, Surely he is torn in pieces; and I saw him not since: And if ye take this also from me, and mischief befall him, ye shall bring down my gray hairs with sorrow to the grave. Now therefore when I come to thy servant my father, and the lad be not with us; seeing that his life is bound up in the lad's life; it shall come to pass, when he seeth that the lad is not with us, that he will die: and thy servants shall bring down the gray hairs of thy servant our father with sorrow to the grave. For thy servant became surety for the lad unto my father, saying, If I bring him not unto thee, then I shall bear the blame to my father forever. Now therefore, I pray thee, let thy servant abide instead of the lad a bondman to my lord;

and let the lad go up with his brethren. For how shall I go up to my father, and the lad be not with me? lest peradventure I see the evil that shall come on my father.

Here ends the counsel for the defense. How must Benjamin and the brethren have felt when they heard noble Judah argue his case, point by point, before the governor! With what admiration they beheld him, for surely the lord of the land must have a heart of stone to resist such forceful pleading. They were soon to know that it had done its work and had accomplished its purpose.

Before proceeding, let us notice some of the details that display the eloquence and shattering power of Judah's irresistible speech:

Seven times he speaks of himself as "thy servant."

Fourteen times he mentions the "father."

Four times he refers to the father as "thy servant."

Once he describes him as an "old man."

Once he spoke of Benjamin's mother.

Three times he speaks of Benjamin as the "youngest brother."

Once Benjamin is referred to as the "child of the father's old age."

Once Benjamin is spoken of as "a little one."

Thirteen times Benjamin is called "the lad."

Once he said "his brother is dead."

About this brother, the "father believed he was torn in pieces."

Twice he told of bringing down "his gray hairs with sorrow to the grave."

Twice he warns the governor concerning the danger of his father's death, should they go back without Benjamin.

He said, his father's life was "bound up in the lad's life."

As surety he said, "Let thy servant abide instead of the lad a bondman . . . and let the lad go up with his brethren."

161

> Last of all, seeming to be at breaking point again,
> he cries, *"How shall I go up to my father, and
> the lad be not with me? lest peradventure I see
> the evil that shall come on my father."*

One can imagine Joseph's reaction. He might have
asked, "Can this be the same Judah, willing now to
sell his own life into slavery for his little half-brother?"
What a change of mind and heart was evident, from
the day he with his brethren sold him into slavery and
broke their father's heart! To get him out of the way
was their only concern that day. Motivated by jealousy
as cruel as the grave, they parted with him regardless
of the consequences. Judah's earnest and weighty appeal now ended, brings us to the great crisis of this
historic drama, and reveals Joseph's strategy in bringing
these guilty brethren to their knees, to face up to their
guilty past, and then to experience the joy of reconciliation and full forgiveness.

Before reaching this crisis point, let us look at Judah
as the powerful and victorious advocate. In this capacity he would typify the exalted Lord Jesus Christ
in His present ministry at the right hand of God. Up
there He is not only Priest, but as we shall see He
is also Advocate. In 1 John 2:1 we read, "If any man
sin, we have an advocate with the Father, Jesus Christ
the righteous." The question is asked in Romans 8:34,
"Who is he that condemneth? It is Christ that died,
yea rather, that is risen again, Who is even at the right
hand of God, Who also maketh intercession for us."
The Christian can sing with joy:

> *Before the throne of God above*
> *I have a strong, a perfect plea,*
> *A Great High Priest, whose name is Love,*
> *Who ever lives and pleads for me.*

When Satan tempts me to despair,
Telling of evil yet within,
Upward I look and see Him there,
Who made an end of all my sin.

Indeed there comes to mind now the words of Anne Steele's lovely hymn composed in the seventeenth century:

He lives — the great Redeemer lives;
What joy the blest assurance gives!
And now before His Father, God,
Pleads the full merit of His blood.

Great Advocate, Almighty Friend,
On Thee do all our hopes depend!
Our cause can never, never fail,
For Thou dost plead, and must prevail.

In every dark, distressing hour,
When sin and Satan join their power,
Let this blest truth repel each dart,
That Thou dost bear us on Thy heart.

Here is encouragement for the penitent sinner as well. John reminds us in the Scripture referred to before that "Jesus Christ the righteous . . . is the propitiation [or mercy seat] for our sins: and not for ours only, but also for the sins of the whole world." Let the sinner come before God in acknowledgment of his sin and guilt, plead the merit of Christ's atoning blood, then the great Advocate will take up his case, and God for Christ's sake, based upon the finished work of Calvary, will speak the word of pardoning grace.

The story is told of an Alpine guide who, having gone round a dangerous ledge, put out his hand to the leader of the party, but the man hesitated and seemed reluctant to move, for a yawning chasm lay beneath. The guide, much annoyed, said to the apprehensive

163

man, "Come!" Again stretching out his hand to him he said, "There's a hand that never lost a man." How true this is of our Heavenly Advocate! We might say of Him, "There is an Advocate who never failed a client." Put your case in His hand, sinner, you who are in need of mercy and pardon, for "He is able also to save them to the uttermost that come unto God by Him" (Heb. 7:25).

Every word of Judah's pleading pierced Joseph's heart, and he deeply felt the distress of his own mother's son standing silent before him, bearing the load of an undeserved accusation. He was now fully convinced of their change of mind by the care the men had for Benjamin. He could also read their earnest desire to spare the old father a further trial that would put him in his grave. He was convinced, as well, that never again would they act as they did when they tore from him "the coat of many colors" at Dothan, for there they were completely unconcerned as to their father's feelings, and the burden of sorrow that was to crush his broken spirit for years to come. Mr. Lawson, a writer of the last century, says, "Joseph's heart was strongly agitated by the tenderest and most powerful passions, filial and fraternal love, compassion, joy, and grief" *(Lawson's History of Joseph, page 253).*

CHAPTER 31

THE REVELATION

"Then Joseph could not refrain himself before all them that stood by him; and he cried, Cause every man to go out from me. And there stood no man with him, while Joseph made himself known unto his brethren. And he wept aloud: and the Egyptians and the house of Pharaoh heard. And Joseph said unto his brethren, 'I am Joseph; doth my father yet live?' And his brethren could not answer him; for they were troubled at his presence" (Gen. 45:1-3).

Let us consider first of all Joseph's command: "Cause every man to go out from me." This session had to be in camera. Had the servants been allowed to stay, they would have learned the shameful treatment their lord had received at the hands of these men, and no doubt would have been enraged at the thought of forgiveness being extended to them. No, Joseph would not expose them and have their sin proclaimed from the housetops. Love covers a multitude of sins (1 Peter 4:8; Prov. 10:12).

This act of Joseph is again eminently typical of the Saviour of men, exalted at God's right hand, seated in the place of honor and glory, who waits and longs to speak the word of forgiveness to the repentant sinner. Will He make a public display of his guilty past? Will He blazen it abroad, that all might hear to the embarrassment of the confessor? Far from it, He will see to it that His ear alone will hear the sinner's confession, and having heard it, will send him on his way, blotting out, as a thick cloud, his transgressions, and, as a cloud, his sins (Isa. 44:22).

Making this a private interview shows Joseph's consideration for his erring brethren, but another reason why he caused every man to go from him was that he was strained to the utmost emotionally. The floodgate of his tears was about to burst open, and this must not be as the lord of the land before his servants. He was indeed Zaphnath-paaneah, the *saviour* of the land, the saviour of his father's house as well; but here he is weeping. Shall we say, a weeping saviour? In fact, we read, "He wept aloud"; they heard him, but they were not allowed to see him.

We go in thought again to the Saviour who is Christ the Lord. We fix our eyes on these two words of John 11:35: *"Jesus wept."* No doubt He was moved at the devastation which sin had wrought also at the sight of brokenhearted sisters and the dread tomb with its corruption which confronted Him. The Jews around Him were weeping. His tears were tears of human sympathy, but they were more than that: they were tears of grief for a world upon which rested the weight of the dark shadow of death. Jerusalem was ignorant of the fact that the coming of our Lord into the world meant for them the day of visitation. The Lord knew that soon outside Jerusalem's wall He would be crucified and slain. He also knew the day in the near future when their city would be left a heap of rubble by the invading Roman army, and knowing this "He beheld the city, and wept over it" (Luke 19:41). Indeed, the sense of the word is, He literally wailed.

How true of Him were the words spoken by Jehovah in the Old Testament, "I have no pleasure in the death of the wicked" (Ezek. 33:11). Hebrews 5:7 shows the blessed Saviour again praying and supplicating, this time "with strong crying and tears unto

Him that was able to save Him out of death, and was heard in that He feared." Here we have the tears of Gethsemane and Calvary. It is impossible for us to enter into these realms of deepest sorrow and unutterable grief. How true it is what Sankey sang:

> *None of the ransomed ever knew*
> *How deep were the waters crossed.*

With what gladness the Christian sings today:

> *'Tis past, the dark and dreary night,*
> *And, Lord, we hail Thee now,*
> *Our Morning Star, without a cloud*
> *Of sadness on Thy brow.*

How comforting in the hour of sorrow to remember, when our Lord Jesus went up on high, He carried with Him His perfect manhood, and so He is able to enter into the sorrows of His own, and can "be touched with the feeling of our infirmities [for He] was in all points tried like as we are, yet without sin" (Heb. 4:15).

Now for the startling revelation. As the confused brethren stand looking at the governor of the land, convulsed with grief, wailing aloud, little did they dream what would be the result of this private interview. His weeping over, he seems to look steadfastly at them for a moment. Then come these words with shattering effect, "I AM JOSEPH." Indeed, the "am" is in italics, so we have but two words, "I JOSEPH." I think it is impossible for anyone to describe how these two words affected these men! How dumb-struck were the ten who had torn "the coat of many colors" from off his back, and put him in the slave market so many years before! What a moment for the lad Benjamin! Actually now looking into the eyes of his real brother, whom he thought had been torn to pieces by some fierce animal. What a revelation this was to him!

167

After Joseph made himself known, his first question was, "Doth my father yet live?" But they could not answer him, for they were terrified at his presence. What a word is this, "Terrified at his presence"! I just cannot pass this without looking on to that dreadful day when impenitent sinners shall be summoned to stand before the Lord Jesus Christ when He sits as Judge at the great final assize —

> *When they from out their lonely tomb,*
> *Shall stand in Judgment's awful doom.*

At the very sight of the Judge's face the heavens and the earth shall flee away. Will it be the face that was marred at Gabbatha and Golgotha? Yes, the same face! It is the Christ of the Tree, that is Judge on the Throne.

> *Oh, awful day, who would not be*
> *Sheltered, O Lamb of God, in Thee,*
> *Safe at Thy side when, wild and loud,*
> *The shrieks of that unnumbered crowd*
> *Shall rend the heavens and fill the skies,*
> *Till judgment's doom shall close their cries!*

I pray earnestly that none who read this will find themselves arraigned before that Great White Throne. Seek shelter in Christ now for "There is therefore now no condemnation to them which are in Christ Jesus" (Rom. 8:1). The promise of Christ to the believing sinner is, "shall not come into judgment, but is passed from death unto life" (John 5:24).

It would seem the brethren were standing at a distance from Joseph. Of course, it was only right they should do so when they entered his presence, because of his exalted station as Governor of Egypt, and it might be that they even drew farther back at this astounding discovery. Their first thoughts were sure to be, "Now he will have his revenge!" Being in the place of high authority in Egypt, he had the power to retaliate. Joseph could see the visible effect on the horror-stricken faces of the men. They were white with fear, but he quickly allayed these fears by saying, "Come near to me, I pray you."

And they came near, and he said, "I am Joseph your brother, whom ye sold into Egypt. Now therefore be not grieved, nor angry with yourselves, that ye sold me hither: for God did send me before you to preserve life. For these two years hath the famine been in the land: and yet there are five years, in the which there shall neither be earing nor harvest. And God sent me before you to preserve you a posterity in the earth, and to save your lives by a great deliverance. So now it was not you that sent me hither, but God: and He hath made me a father to Pharaoh, and lord of all his house, and a ruler throughout all the land of Egypt" (Gen. 45:4-8).

To these broken and repentant men Joseph unfolds the outworking of the divine plan, and shows that the covenant-keeping God, the God of Abraham, the God in every intervening circumstance, from the day he left Hebron's vale, until he reached the pinnacle of fame in the land of Egypt.

CHAPTER 32

RECONCILIATION AND PARDON

Joseph cleared the ground thus far, and now he says, "Haste ye, and go up to my father, and say unto him, Thus saith thy son Joseph, God hath made me lord of all Egypt: come down unto me, tarry not: And thou shalt dwell in the land of Goshen, and thou shalt be near unto me, thou, and thy children, and thy children's children, and thy flocks, and thy herds, and all that thou hast: And there will I nourish thee; for yet there are five years of famine; lest thou, and thy household, and all that thou hast, come to poverty. And, behold, your eyes see, and the eyes of my brother Benjamin, that it is my mouth that speaketh unto you. And ye shall tell my father of all my glory in Egypt, and of all that ye have seen; and ye shall haste and bring down my father thither" (45:9-13). After these instructions we read one of the most touching incidents in Scripture: "And he fell upon his brother Benjamin's neck, and wept; and Benjamin wept upon his neck. Moreover he kissed all his brethren, and wept upon them: and after that his brethren talked with him" (45:14, 15). We would love to know what they talked about, but it is not given us to know. Here we have what might be termed the *Kiss of Reconciliation*.

In the New Testament the word reconciliation means a thorough change and surely this is what we see here. No longer need the brethren stay afar off; no longer need there be any estrangement for all is changed. Now they are seen in the near place, with all distance removed, and the guilty past wiped out. Joseph and his brethren are one. In 2 Corinthians 5:18-21, reconciliation is based upon the fact of verse 21, "For He [God] hath made Him [Christ] to be sin for us, who knew no sin; that we might be made the righteousness of God in Him." Paul speaks of the Gospel message committed to his trust as the ministry of reconciliation. Verse 17 shows that when a sinner rests on the work of Christ he becomes "a new creature: old things are passed away; behold, all things are become new."

In this sense Joseph again stands out clearly as a type of the Lord Jesus Christ, for as it was Joseph alone who removed the distance, and brought the brethren into the near place, so it is in the antitype. As the brethren did nothing to merit this favor, so it is with the repentant sinner. He has no merit to offer, yet when he rests alone on the work and word of Christ, he can revel in the truth of Ephesians 2:13: "But now in Christ Jesus ye who sometimes were far off are made nigh by the blood of Christ." The following words of the hymn by Philip P. Bliss are full of meaning:

> *"Man of Sorrows!" what a name*
> *For the Son of God who came*
> *Ruined sinners to reclaim!*
> *   Hallelujah! what a Saviour!*
>
> *Bearing shame and scoffing rude,*
> *In my place condemned He stood;*
> *Sealed my pardon with His blood:*
> *   Hallelujah! what a Saviour!*
>
> *Guilty, vile, and helpless, we;*
> *Spotless Lamb of God was He:*
> *"Full atonement," can it be?*
> *   Hallelujah! what a Saviour!*

171

Lifted up was He to die,
"It is finished," was His cry;
Now in Heaven exalted high:
   Hallelujah! what a Saviour!

The secret meeting now over, reconciliation effected, and the identity of Joseph's brethren fully established, the news spread to Pharaoh's house, "Joseph's brethren are come," and we read, "it pleased Pharaoh well, and his servants."

CHAPTER 33

JOSEPH'S BOUNTY

Joseph was summoned into the presence of Pharaoh, "And Pharaoh said unto Joseph, 'Say unto thy brethren, This do ye; lade your beasts, and go, get you unto the land of Canaan; and take your father and your households, and come unto me: and I will give you the good of the land of Egypt, and ye shall eat the fat of the land. Now thou art commanded, this do ye; take you wagons out of the land of Egypt for your little ones, and for your wives, and bring your father and come. Also regard not your stuff; for the good of all the land of Egypt is yours.' And the children of Israel did so: and Joseph gave them wagons, according to the commandment of Pharaoh, and gave them provision for the way. To all of them Joseph gave each man changes of raiment; but to Benjamin he gave three hundred pieces of silver, and five changes of raiment. And to his father he sent after this manner; ten asses laden with the good things of Egypt, and ten she asses laden with corn and bread and meat for his father by the way. So he sent his brethren away, and they departed: and he said unto them, 'See that ye fall not out by the way' " (Gen. 45:17-24).

What a royal send-off! Who could believe it? What a sight to see these men going out laden with the good things of Egypt, given by Pharaoh for Joseph's sake! Not only were they forgiven, reconciled, and the black past blotted out, but they were also made partakers of Joseph's rich bounty, and had Pharaoh's promise of a new home in the land of plenty, even though five years of famine still lay ahead. Such bountiful treatment, received on the top of pardoning mercy, has surely a Gospel ring about it. Romans 8:32 asks the question, "He that spared not His own Son, but delivered Him up for us all, how shall He not with Him also freely give us all things?" Ephesians 1:3 tells the Christian that he is blessed with all spiritual blessings in the heavenlies *in Christ*. In 1 Peter 1:3-4 we read, "Blessed be the God and Father of our Lord Jesus Christ, which according to His abundant mercy hath begotten us again unto a lively [living] hope by the resurrection of Jesus Christ from the dead, to an inheritance incorruptible, and undefiled, and that fadeth not away, reserved in heaven for you."

Great and abundant were the supplies they carried home to their old father and their families, but towering above all this was the prospect of a new home in Goshen with its plenty. And more than that, Joseph said, "Thou shalt be near unto me." I cannot pass this without thinking, not only of the blessings the Christians are loaded with now, and the provision for the rest of the way, but of the glorious prospect of a home in Heaven, and the eternal joy of "being near" to our Heavenly "Joseph." "To dwell with Him, to see His face," the face of our Eternal Lover, "once marred more than any man's," but in that day it will be as the "sun shineth in his strength." When the Christian lays hold of this blessed hope, it makes him a "pilgrim and a stranger" here below, and causes him to have many a longing for the "Homeland."

I recall crossing the Atlantic toward home from the United States of America in the great ship *S. S. America*. We were nearing our destiny when a voice rang out through the public address system saying that in half an hour we would be in sight of Land's End. I can

174

never forget the rush to the side of the great vessel, especially the eager and concentrated gaze of the older folks, some of whom had been away on foreign soil for years. The binoculars were out to catch the first glimpse of home! For them it was home, even though for years they had been separated from it by three thousand miles of water. Just as the half hour had gone, there on the horizon lay the longed-for shores of England. I could hear some say, "Look, there it is!" while others shed tears of joy, and said one to another, "We'll soon be there!" Others struck up old-time songs of home. I tell you it was a moving scene.

Does my reader have this happy and bright prospect of Heaven's eternal home and of sharing its never-fading joys with all the redeemed, where the Lamb is all the glory? What a blessed future for the Christian is recorded in Revelation 22:3-5: "And there shall be no more curse: but the throne of God and of the Lamb shall be in it; and His servants shall serve Him: And they shall see His face; and His name shall be in their foreheads. And there shall be no night there."

Reader, how sad it would be to miss Heaven! Only those will be there who have put a personal faith and trust in Christ, and have known His pardoning grace. Such have their names written in "The Lamb's book of life." Is your name written there? One of the most tragic sights described by the Saviour is in Luke 13:25-28. Visualize that vast, unnumbered crowd, outside the closed door of Heaven, knocking and saying, "Lord, Lord, open unto us"; and He shall answer and say unto them, "I know you not whence ye are." Although they protest saying, "We have eaten and drunk in Thy presence, and Thou hast taught in our streets," the Lord answers, "I tell you, I know you not whence ye are; depart from Me, all ye workers of iniquity. There shall be weeping and gnashing of teeth, when ye shall see Abraham, and Isaac, and Jacob, and all the prophets, in the kingdom of God, and you yourselves thrust out."

> *God's house is filling fast,*
>   *"Yet there is room!"*
> *Some soul will be the last,*
>   *"Yet there is room!"*
>
> *Yes! soon salvation's day*
> *From you will pass away,*
> *Then grace no more will say —*
>   *"Yet there is room!"*

Reader, if you have not yet made sure your title to the great eternal home in Heaven, I beg of you, do it now, by a personal acceptance of Christ as Surety, Saviour, and Lord.

In Genesis 45:24 we see the great procession set out for home. We read that Joseph "sent his brethren away , . . . and he said unto them, See that ye fall not out by the way." These last words of his are surely most striking — "See that ye fall not out by the way." The many human touches in this story make it so true to life. It is not easy for eleven brothers not to have a falling-out about something, and, of course, surely a very embarrassing time lay ahead of them. If the old father should ask how did Joseph get to Egypt in the first place, when he had only sent him to Shechem to seek their welfare; and if he should ask why they had brought to him the "coat of many colors," soaked in blood, how would they answer? Would all the families have to get to know their cruel, heartless treatment of Joseph, and their wicked deception in the case of old Jacob? We are kept in the dark as to what transpired on the way home. At any rate there is no record of them having fallen out by the way.

176

CHAPTER 34

THE HOMECOMING

Before the brethren left Egypt, instead of stripping them of their coats, Joseph gave each of them a change of raiment, and to Benjamin, far from taking his coat, he gave five changes of raiment. In that earlier day, the brethren sold Joseph for twenty pieces of silver, but this day he gives Benjamin three hundred pieces of silver — fifteen times the amount for which Joseph was sold. Surely this beneficent treatment was convincing proof of Joseph's full and free forgiveness.

The Scripture next records: "And they went up out of Egypt, and came into the land of Canaan unto Jacob their father" (Gen. 45:25). How often I have tried to visualize the scene of their arrival and see them stand, first of all, before their old father! What a contrast from the time they stood before him on their return from Dothan, only to spread before him Joseph's "coat of many colors," and Judah with the price of a slave in his bag, knowing while they stood there that the lad was on his way to the slave market in Egypt. What throbbing hearts there must have been as they came in sight of the vale of Hebron!

From the father's home, too, we can imagine many a look had been cast in the direction of Egypt, and especially after what had happened on the first visit. At that time they came home without Simeon, but on this occasion they come home with Simeon and the lad Benjamin. The families, during their absence, would be wondering and asking themselves if the lord of the land, who treated them at the first so roughly, and accused them of being spies, would treat them differently, on account of the fact that Benjamin was now with them. As to their arrival, though we are not told, no doubt Hebron would be astir as the great caravan appeared in the distance. Shall I say they could well have been filled with fear, for not only could they detect the men and the asses, but whose were the wagons? Whose were these? Can we picture some of the younger folks running on to meet the strange procession? When near enough they make account of the men and the asses, and we hear them cry, "They are all there!" Then they meet, fathers and children, and fall into each other's embrace. What a welcome for Simeon, and for the lad Benjamin! The journey completed, the brethren find the vale of Hebron waiting to give them a joyous welcome. From the day they left with Benjamin to go to Egypt for more food, the homes of the men had been gripped with the deepest concern for their success and safe return. Now fear and concern was all over, and no doubt many thanksgivings went up to the God of Jacob for His protecting and preserving care.

The first recorded words of the men were spoken as they stood in the presence of Jacob. These were words which put the old patriarch into a state of absolute bewilderment and confusion, especially the first four words, "Joseph is yet alive." The words that followed only added to his bewilderment, for they conveyed to him what seemed utterly impossible — "and he is governor over all the land of Egypt." What else could be expected of the old man who for years had mourned the loss of his darling Joseph? Did he not with his own two eyes see the lad's "coat of many colors" soaked with blood? And did he not recall how he had waited in vain for his return? Had they told him that Abraham and Isaac had risen from the dead, he scarcely could have been more surprised. If Joseph was alive, how was it he had allowed twenty years to pass without making an effort to get news to his father

178

who had been mourning his loss for all these years? Surely it was also hard for him to imagine a despised Hebrew filling the place of governor in the great land of Egypt, and next to Pharaoh on the throne. No wonder we read, "Jacob's heart fainted, for he believed them not."

At this point of the story again the Lord Jesus Christ, the great Antitype comes to mind, for when His disciples were told by Mary Magdalene He was alive, and had been seen by her, they believed not. Luke tells us, when the women returning from the sepulchre gave the apostles the news, their words seemed like idle tales, and they believed them not. Later, when Jesus Himself appeared, stood in their midst, and showed them His hands and His feet, "they believed not for joy, and wondered." The news seemed too good to be true without surer evidence than is required for ordinary events.

This is how Jacob was affected. Indeed, the report agitated his mind to such a degree that his old frame could not sustain the shock, for there seemed to be certain proofs both that Joseph was dead, and that he was not dead. The one moment he accepted the fact that his loved son was alive, the next he doubted if it could be so. To him there was an air of mystery about the whole affair. As the message from Joseph was fully told, it was impossible for them to hide how Joseph got to Egypt. It involved their sinful act in selling him for a slave and taking back the blood-stained "coat of many colors" to cover up their foul deed. What a revelation this would be to old Jacob! Would he not feel like turning from them forever? Evidently this is not how he felt. Instead, as he looked at the wagons that were sent for himself and his house, his spirit revived; and he said, "It is enough; Joseph is yet alive: I will go and see him before I die."

179

CHAPTER 35

ISRAEL THE MAN OF FAITH

As Israel, the man of faith, Jacob comes to the fore-front, recognizing that the hand of the covenant-keeping God could be traced in the whole matter, from beginning to end. Not so long ago as a heart-broken man, thinking of Joseph as gone, never to return, he had wailed, "All these things are against me." From the burial of his beloved Rachel, it seemed to be just one blow after another. I doubt if there is a Christian anywhere, but knows something of Jacob's experience. We all have encountered times when the going is hard, when one trial is hardly past, then another is following hard on its heels.

Early in my Christian life I attended a conference at Leith. One of the speakers that day was the late Mr. James Moffit of Glasgow, a most able servant of Christ. He had been passing through deep waters, yet he took his place before the saints and delivered the Lord's message with great feeling. Speaking on the subject of God-sent trials, he gave an exhortation that has lived with me ever since. He said, "When you are brought into trial, do not ask God to take you out of it, rather ask Him for grace to keep you, while you are in it, so that when He does bring you out of it, you will have acquired a deeper and greater knowledge of Himself."

E. P. Hammond tells of a Liverpool lad, who went to bathe, and found himself carried out with the tide. Though he struggled long and hard, he was not able to swim against the ebbing tide, with the result he was carried out to sea. He was picked up by a boat bound for Dublin. The poor little lad was almost lost. The sailors were all very kind to him and got him clothed. That very evening a gentleman who was walking near the place where the boy had gone in to swim, found his clothes lying on the shore. He found a piece of paper in the lad's coat by which he discovered to whom the clothes belonged. The kind man with a very heavy heart went to break the news to the parents. He said to the father, "I'm very sorry to tell you, I found these clothes on the shore and could not find the lad to whom they belonged. I almost fear he has been drowned."

The father could not speak. He was so overcome with grief; the mother was wild with sorrow. They caused every possible inquiry to be made, but no account was to be had of the missing boy. It was a sad house, and the little children missed their play-fellow. Mourning was ordered; the mother spent her time crying, and the father was silent in his grief. He said little but felt more than words could express. The lad was transferred in Dublin to a ship bound for Liverpool, and it arrived on the day on which the mourning had to be held with all the friends. As soon as he reached Liverpool, not wanting to be seen in the strange outfit given him by the sailors, he made his way home through the by-lanes where no one would recognize him. At last he came to the hall door and knocked. When the servant opened it, she screamed with joy and shouted to the gathered mourners, "Here is master Tom!" The father rushed to the door, and, bursting into tears, embraced him. The mother fainted, being completely overcome. This put an end to the mourning. The father could say, like Jacob, "It is enough; my son is yet alive."

To go to Egypt would mean a long and tiring journey for an old and worn man, but the thought of seeing

181

the face of Joseph outweighed for Jacob the thought of all the dangers and hardships of the way.

I recall a meeting in Boston at the end of which I was shaking hands with the audience as they dispersed. A fine looking man took my hand; I noticed he was blind. I asked him if he was always blind, and he answered, "I was born blind, and I am glad, for the first face I shall ever see will be the face of my Saviour." I may tell you I was greatly moved, to think that for this dear Christian to see the Saviour's face seemed to outweigh for him the life-long trial of his physical affliction. Maud Frazer in her beautiful hymn strikes the same note of expectancy:

> *Satisfied my highest longing,*
> *Earthly griefs as naught shall be,*
> *When I wake with Christ in glory,*
> *When His face I see.*
>
> *Though ofttimes the way He leadeth,*
> *Is a way of mystery,*
> *There shall be no gloom or sadness,*
> *When His face I see.*
>
> *When His face I see,*
> *When His face I see,*
> *Oh, the joy for me awaiting,*
> *When His face I see.*

Despite all the sorrows and heartbreaks Jacob had known, since the loss of his beloved Rachel and the disappearance of Joseph, also the long and tiresome journey to Egypt that lay before him, the very thought of seeing the face of Joseph made up for it all. On the brethren's arrival home, to have the lad Benjamin again in his embrace would have been sufficient to satisfy and comfort the aged patriarch. But now he has grasped the fact that Joseph is yet alive, and what will he not do, suffer, or risk, to obtain another sight of Rachel's firstborn, not now wearing the "coat of many colors," but robed as the governor of all Egypt? The hitherto un-dreamed-of prospect completely mastered him. His attitude to Joseph's brethren also, despite what they had done to Joseph, was one of forgiveness, for he would reason, if Joseph, the one whom they had really wronged had forgiven them, he must of necessity do the same.

Considering Jacob's inward joy and delight at the thought of seeing the face of Joseph, brought me to think of old Jasper, the renowned colored preacher, who when he was dying fell into a sleep and began to dream. His faithful and lifelong partner sitting at his bedside said to him as he wakened, "Jasper, you dream-ing, for you smile in your sleep?" "Yes, honey," he replied, 'I dreamed I was at de gate of Hebben, and a shining angel says to me, 'Have you got your passport, Jasper?' I said, 'Yes, de blood o' Christ,' and he said, 'Come on in.' He said to me when inside, 'Jasper, would you like to see Moses?' I said, 'To be sure.' Again he asked, 'What about Elijah?' I said, 'Oh, yes, but angel, first take me to where Jesus is, and don't disturb me for a million years.' " Blind Fanny Crosby was living in the good of the same blessed prospect when she wrote:

When my lifework is ended and I cross the swelling tide,
  When the bright and glorious morning I shall see;
I shall know my Redeemer when I reach the other side,
  And His smile will be the first to welcome me.

Thro' the gates of the city in a robe of spotless white,
  He will lead me where no tears will ever fall;
In the glad song of ages I shall mingle with delight,
  But I long to meet my Saviour first of all.

Going back in thought for a moment to Joseph's words to the brethren, "Ye shall tell my father of all

183

my glory in Egypt, and of all that ye have seen" (Gen. 45:13), carries us on to the New Testament again. The Lord Jesus Christ, whom His own nation rejected and eventually crucified, has come out of the tomb, and has showed Himself alive after His passion by many infallible proofs, being seen of His disciples forty days, and speaking of the things pertaining to the Kingdom of God. After our Lord's ascension to glory, we find Peter standing up with the eleven on the Day of Pentecost (Acts 2:22). He charges the nation of Israel with their guilt in crucifying Jesus of Nazareth, the Man approved of God, and at the same time he emphasizes that behind their guilty act, was the determinate counsel and foreknowledge of God. Then he adds, "Whom God hath raised up, having loosed the pains of death." He then goes on to show how in raising Christ from the dead, it is God who does so in fulfillment of the Old Testament prophecies, and also to prove His acceptance of Christ's atoning sacrifice made at Calvary. Then Peter, in an outburst of triumph, cries, "Therefore let all the house of Israel know assuredly, that God hath made that same Jesus, whom ye have crucified, both Lord and Christ" (v. 36).

How clear is the Antitype! Joseph was sold by his own brethren for the price of a slave, and humiliated, "until the iron entered his soul" (Psalm 105:18). He was numbered with the transgressors, treated as guilty though actually innocent, then elevated from the lowest place to the highest, there to become the lord and saviour of the land. Surely all this points to the One we have just considered, for all this was true in an infinitely greater degree of Christ, the Heavenly Joseph. He was once crowned with thorns on the cross, but is now crowned with glory and honor; once He filled the lowest place on earth, but now He fills the highest place in Heaven.

CHAPTER 36

FAREWELL TO SHECHEM

How long it took Jacob and all the families to make ready for their departure to Egypt we are not told. Chapter 46:1 just begins, "And Israel took his journey with all that he had, and came to Beer-sheba, and offered sacrifices unto the God of his father Isaac."

It is significant to note that it was as Israel, not as Jacob, that he took his journey. It was indeed the same Jacob, but it is his princely name that is used, for he is now again in the path of faith. He has seen clearly by now that, through all the vicissitudes of the past twenty years, the covenant-keeping God was working out His own plan and purpose, and that, for the good of His chosen people.

Beer-sheba is the first stopping place mentioned. The name signifies, "The well of the oath." It was first given to the place where Abraham and Abimelech made a covenant not to molest each other, and confirmed it by an oath. It afterwards became the dwelling place of Abraham and Isaac who dug a well there. In Genesis 21:33 we read, "And Abraham planted a grove in Beer-sheba, and called there on the name of the Lord, the everlasting God." The very name, Beer-sheba, held sacred memories for old Jacob. It was there he parted from his father and mother, and from the angry face of his brother Esau so many years before. He went out like his grandfather, Abraham, not knowing whither he went. He knew what his destination was, but as to the success of his journey and all that lay between, he was totally in the dark. However, on that occasion, as the first day's journey ended, he reached Luz, which to him became Bethel, the House of God. Here I would be tempted to stay a while, for what a story is attached to Bethel in Genesis 28!

The Bible reader will recall, it was there that Jacob had the memorable dream of the "ladder set up on the earth, and the top of it reached to heaven" (v. 12). It was there the Lord spoke to Jacob saying, "I am the Lord God of Abraham thy father, and the God of Isaac: the land whereon thou liest, to thee will I give it, and to thy seed; and thy seed shall be as the dust of the earth, and thou shalt spread abroad to the west, and to the east, and to the north, and to the south: and in thee and in thy seed shall all the families of the earth be blessed. And, behold, I am with thee, and will keep thee in all places whither thou goest, and will bring thee again in this land; for I will not leave thee, until I have done that which I have spoken to thee of" (vv. 13-15). Is it any wonder the old patriarch wanted to halt at Beer-sheba? Was the word falling on his ear again, "I am with thee, and will keep thee in all places whither thou goest"? and this for Jacob included Egypt.

Arriving at Beer-sheba, he offered sacrifices unto the God of his father Isaac. According to the patriarchal rite, it was in order for Jacob to do priestly work, for although he was the second man, he was by divine arrangement the firstborn of Isaac, and as we emphasized at the beginning of the book, this honor was the portion of the firstborn in those days. It seems that Jacob could not pass this place of hallowed memory, without getting near to this God whose promise given that night so long ago had never failed. In the recent past his spiritual perception had been quickened to recognize how the hand of God had been working for his good over these years of deep and sore trial, when he thought everything was against him. How clearly does Jacob's halting at Beer-sheba bring to the fore Israel, the man of faith, and at the same time his utter dependence on God that he might have His guidance and blessing for the hitherto untrodden path.

Humanly speaking, he had grave cause for concern. Not only did there lie before him a hazardous journey, but this was a complete breaking with his former life. Hebron with all its treasured associations must be left behind to settle in another country, and of all places, Egypt. Too well he remembered a day in his father's history, when there was a famine in the land (Gen. 26:2, 3), when he cast an eye on Egypt, but God forbade him, saying, "Go not down into Egypt; dwell in the land which I shall tell thee of: sojourn in this land, and I will be with thee, and will bless thee." Could not this be one of the chief reasons why in his petitions, and in the offering up of his sacrifices he appealed to the God of his father Isaac? He would surely reason thus, if God forbade my father Isaac, in whom were vested the promises, from going down to Egypt, why am I now heading in that direction?

CHAPTER 37

JACOB PROVES GOD AT BEER-SHEBA

Jacob wanted to have assurance that the excursion into Egypt was in line with the will of his God. This certainly was expected of Jacob. He had indeed said he would go to Egypt before leaving Shechem, but as the man of faith, he never attempted to journey unless he had divine approval. How he longed to see the face of Joseph! What a thrill this prospect gave him! Nevertheless, his conduct at Beer-sheba indicates that he would rather die without seeing him than be outside the path of God's will. We could say that Jacob was acting on the precept of Proverbs 3:6, "In all thy ways acknowledge Him," and counting upon the attached promise, "and He shall direct thy paths." His approaching God, as the God of his father Isaac, links his movements with the concept of the Abrahamic covenant. It was to Abraham God gave the promises of an innumerable seed, and possession of Palestine "from the Euphrates to the Nile, the river of Egypt." Isaac, being the son of promise and Abraham's heir, was directly associated with the covenant promises. That is why we have recurring again and again the expression, "The God of Abraham, Isaac and Jacob."

No doubt Jacob could remember having heard his father Isaac speak of Abraham's faith and love toward God, and of the mercy and truth which God showed him during his long life of pilgrimage. Nevertheless, it is evident that so much of the fear of God characterized his own father's life, that it made an indelible impression on Jacob's mind and regulated his movements throughout the years of his life. Twice in Chapter 31 we read of the "fear of his father Isaac." It was at Beer-sheba in Genesis 26:24-25, that the Lord appeared to Isaac his father, and said unto him, "I am the God of Abraham thy father: fear not, for I am with thee, and will bless thee, and multiply thy seed, for My servant Abraham's sake," and Jacob built an altar there, and called upon the name of the Lord.

Here at Beer-sheba we should learn from Jacob's attitude, one of the most important lessons to be learned by the Christian while journeying on to his prospective home in Heaven. Surely it is the need for ascertaining the will of God, especially when important decisions have to be made, decisions that could affect the whole of one's future life — its usefulness and testimony. How many there are who look back with deepest regret to younger days, when far-off fields seemed green, and human impulse was strong! Decisions were made hurriedly, worldly wisdom carried the day, and, alas, guidance and direction from God were never sought. Last century F. W. Faber wrote:

> *I bow me to Thy will, O God,*
> *And all Thy ways adore,*
> *And every day I live I'd seek*
> *To please Thee more and more.*
>
> *He always wins who sides with God,*
> *To him no chance is lost;*
> *God's will is sweetest to him when*
> *It triumphs at his cost.*
>
> *Ill that God blesses is our good,*
> *And unblest good is ill;*
> *And all is right that seems most wrong,*
> *If it be His sweet will.*

189

Let us now consider Jacob's priestly function. "He offered sacrifices unto the God of his father Isaac." From the time of Adam's fall in the garden, the patriarchs made their approach to God by the way of sacrifice. Abel, Noah, Abraham, and many others indicated by so doing their demerit, and their need of pardoning mercy. When we reach the book of Leviticus, we have described to us in detail the features of this way of approach to God. A victim, though ignorant and protesting, had to be slain at the altar. Its blood had to be shed. Before its life was taken the offerer is seen standing with his hand upon its head. It is a sin-offering. It is thus seen identifying himself with his innocent victim. He is confessing, "I am the sinner, and deserve to die." He himself then takes the sacrificial knife and slays his substitute, recognizing it has taken his place and has died in his stead. This done, God says, "His sin shall be forgiven him." Of course, this was but a misty shadow of Calvary's infinite sacrifice. That is the place to which the guilty sinner can repair, identify himself with Calvary's Victim, and leave with the words of God's forgiveness ringing in his ears.

Jacob would be well acquainted with the words of God to Abraham in Genesis 15:13, "And God said unto Abraham, Know of a surety that thy seed shall be a stranger in a land that is not theirs, and shall serve them; and they shall afflict them four hundred years; and also that nation, whom they shall serve, will I judge: and afterward shall they come out with great substance." The land referred to, of course, was Egypt. Did Jacob recognize that his journey was in the divine plan for God's covenant people? Whether or not, he would draw near to God and offer his sacrifices and be assured of God's approval ere he would proceed on his way to Egypt.

Jacob had not long to wait for an answer, for we immediately read, "And God spake unto Israel in the visions of the night, and said, 'Jacob, Jacob.' And he said, 'Here am I.' And He said, 'I am God, the God of thy father: fear not to go down to Egypt; for I will there make of thee a great nation: I will go down with thee into Egypt; and I will also surely bring thee up again: and Joseph shall put his hand upon thine eyes'" (46:2-4). By answering Jacob thus, God renews the covenant with him. When God said, "I am God, the God of thy father," it was equal to saying, "I am what thou ownest Me to be: thou shalt find Me a God with divine wisdom and power engaged for thee; and thou shalt find Me, the God of thy father, true to the covenant made with him."

It seems that old Jacob, upon the first intelligence of Joseph's life and glory in Egypt, resolved without any hesitation to go and see him, yet upon second thought, he saw some difficulties in it, which he did not know how to resolve. The renewing of the covenant, and God's word, "Fear not to go down into Egypt," lifted the burden of uncertainty and anxiety. The next word of God to him, "For I will there make of thee a great nation," was the word given in earlier days to Abraham when the covenant was first made, and this added another assuring note to cheer the heart of the aged pilgrim, for now he could see his part in the plan and purpose of God for Israel His people. God not only promises to go down with him to Egypt, but surely to bring him up again to the land. Jacob laid hold upon that word with firm grasp, as you will find when it came to the time of his death. The last statement of God to him would most certainly stir his emotions: "And Joseph shall put his hand upon thine eyes" (Gen. 46:4).

CHAPTER 38

JUDAH TAKES THE LEAD

We can imagine there would be no unnecessary delay at Beer-sheba. With all seeming obstacles in the mind of the patriarch removed, we read, "And Jacob rose up from Beer-sheba: and the sons of Israel carried Jacob their father, and their little ones, and their wives, in the wagons which Pharaoh had sent to carry him. And they took their cattle, and their goods, which they had gotten in the land of Canaan, and came into Egypt, Jacob, and all his seed with him" (Gen. 46:5-6). After outlining the various families, the sacred historian says, "All the souls of the house of Jacob, which came into Egypt, were three score and ten" (v. 27). This was to be the nucleus of the great nation of which God made mention to Jacob at Beer-sheba.

Now the great and noble Judah comes into prominence again; once more he must fill the first place. He becomes the forerunner of the advancing caravan, for as they were nearing their journey's end, Jacob sent Judah before him unto Joseph, to direct his face unto Goshen. At a later day when the nation was journeying through the wilderness on the way to Canaan, who led the great host then? Of course it was Judah! One can almost picture his standard with the lion fluttering in the breeze. When, much later, the day for the occupation of Canaan arrived " . . . the children of Israel asked the Lord saying, Who shall go up for us against the Canaanites first, to fight against them? And the Lord said, Judah shall go up: behold, I have delivered the land into his hand" (Judges 1:1, 2). When Judah leads the caravan into Egypt, the land of promise, he becomes a lovely type of our Lord Jesus Christ, of whom we read in Hebrews 2:10, that He is the Captain of Salvation bringing many sons unto glory.

Looking again at the great host marching through the wilderness led by the standard of Judah, our eye is directed to the Church's march through the wilderness of this world, with the Lord Jesus Christ as the great File-leader. Indeed, in Hebrews 6, we as Christians are seen as having "fled for refuge to lay hold upon the hope set before us: which hope we have as an anchor of the soul, both sure and stedfast, and which entereth into that within the veil; whither the Forerunner is for us entered, even Jesus" (vv. 18-20). In Judges 1, to which we have referred, it was the matter of conquest. There Judah was in the first place again, thus reminding us of Revelation 5:4, 5 where Christ is seen about to subjugate the nations of men, and make His enemies the footstool of His feet. A book containing the hardening judgments which were ready to be poured out on a world of rebellious sinners, was produced, but alas, it was sealed with seven seals. "No man in heaven, nor in earth, neither under the earth, was able to open the book, neither to look thereon." John who saw this in the vision, wept because of it; then one came to John saying, "Weep not: behold, the Lion of the tribe of Judah, the Root of David, hath prevailed to open the book, and to loose the seven seals thereof." And who was the Lion of the tribe of Judah? None other than the Lamb freshly slain, standing in the midst of the throne. So in these different aspects of Judah's conduct, our minds are carried forward to think of our Lord Jesus Christ as the Captain of our Salvation, The Great File-Leader, The Forerunner, The Universal Conqueror.

193

CHAPTER 39

MEETING THE FATHER

On Judah's arrival, Joseph wasted no time, but "made ready his chariot, and went up to meet Israel his father, to Goshen, and presented himself unto him; and he fell on his neck, and wept on his neck a good while. And Israel said unto Joseph, 'Now let me die, since I have seen thy face, because thou art yet alive'" (Gen. 46:29, 30). After these twenty long years of separation, to describe the joy that Joseph felt and gave when he saw the face of his dearly-loved father would be an impossible task for any of us. Before he could find words to express his joy, he told it out by his tears. What a moving sight to see Joseph lying on old Jacob's neck weeping his heart out, and this he did for a good while! To tell the feelings of joy that filled the heart of the father, as he held tightly to his breast his long-lost son, would likewise be vain and hopeless. For years he had mourned for him as dead, and had intended to carry his grief with him to the grave, but now his face is damp from the flowing tears of that very son — yes, his very own Joseph who one day long ago was as the apple of his eye as he moved about the vale of Hebron wearing the "coat of many colors"!

This touching episode over, and the tears of joy now dried, Joseph speaks the word of welcome. Though Jacob had said to Joseph, "Now let me die, since I have seen thy face, because thou art yet alive," little did he know that God was going to give him seventeen years of Joseph's company, before earth's terminus would be reached. He was to have seventeen years more in which to rejoice and be glad in the kindness and faithfulness of the covenant-keeping God, the God of Abraham, and of his father Isaac!

Joseph tells the brethren and their households that he would go up to Pharaoh and acquaint him of their arrival, and he would tell him also the nature of their business, and that they had brought their flocks and their herds with them. This would let Pharaoh know that they were not coming as beggars to impose upon his goodness, but rather they were coming to sojourn and engage in their trade and business, for indeed they had sprung from a race of shepherds, this making them most appreciative of his goodness in giving them a home in Goshen. Five of the brethren are selected to appear with Joseph before Pharaoh. The first question he asked was, "What is your occupation?" and they answered as Joseph had instructed them, and expressed their desire to dwell in the land of Goshen, since every shepherd is an abomination unto the Egyptians. Pharaoh replied to Joseph, "The land of Egypt is before thee; in the land of Goshen let them dwell." Then Joseph brought in his old father, and Jacob blessed Pharaoh. "And Pharaoh said unto Jacob, 'How old art thou?' And Jacob said unto Pharaoh, 'The days of the years of my pilgrimage are an hundred and thirty years: few and evil have the days of the years of my life been, and have not attained unto the days of the years of the life of my fathers in the days of their pilgrimage.' And Jacob blessed Pharaoh, and went out from before Pharaoh. And Joseph placed his father and his brethren, and gave them a possession in the land of Egypt, in the best of the land, in the land of Rameses, as Pharaoh had commanded" (Gen. 47:8-11).

195

All the good that came to Jacob and his sons with their families from the hand of Pharaoh was all because of Joseph. It was really for his sake that they were so blessed. Here we see a beautiful New Testament principle. In Ephesians 1:3-7 the Christian is seen "blessed . . . with all spiritual blessings in heavenly places in Christ." He is chosen in Him, given the position of sonship, accepted in the Beloved One, redeemed and forgiven according to the riches of His grace, and all this because of his union with the Lord Jesus Christ.

The answer Jacob gave to Pharaoh concerning his age is most significant. He said, "The days of the years of my pilgrimage are an hundred and thirty years." When his grandfather Abraham was called by God to leave his country and his kindred we read, "He went out, not knowing whither he went." From that day his life became a pilgrimage. Hebrews 11 records: "By faith he sojourned in the land of promise, as in a strange country, dwelling in tents with Isaac and Jacob, the heirs with him of the same promise" (v. 9). So, like his fathers, Jacob's life was to him as a pilgrimage, for, like Abraham and Isaac, his eye was on the future. "He looked for a city which hath foundations, whose builder and maker is God" (v. 10). These great men were content with their tent and their altar. Peter in his first epistle reminds the Christian that this is his position in the world. He writes in Chapter 2:11, "Dearly beloved, I beseech you as strangers and pilgrims, abstain from fleshly lusts, which war against the soul," and again in 1:17, "Pass the time of your sojourning here in fear." T. R. Taylor grasped this thought early in the last century when he wrote:

> *I'm but a stranger here;*
> *Heaven is my home!*
> *Earth is a desert drear;*
> *Heaven is my home!*

Danger and sorrow stand
Round me on ev'ry hand;
Heav'n is my fatherland,
Heaven is my home!

In the seventy souls that went down into Egypt, Jacob by faith saw the progenitors of a race like the stars of heaven for multitude. The promise made to Abraham and Isaac must stand. A little more than two hundred years ahead, there would be 603,550 men of Jacob's descendants able to go forth to war, in addition to the growing men, mothers and children, also the tribe of Levi solely engaged in the worship and service of God. The promise of God to Jacob at Beer-sheba was that in Egypt he would make of him a great nation.

When we think of the care that Joseph had for his father and his brethren with their families, seeing to it that they lacked nothing but had their every need supplied to the full, it would remind us of Romans 8:32, "He that spared not His own Son, but delivered Him up for us all, how shall He not with Him also freely give us all things?"

CHAPTER 40

JOSEPH THE SAVIOUR

Now that care has been taken of Jacob and the family, the preservation of which was specially designed by divine Providence as seen in Joseph's exaltation and advancement, an account is given of how Joseph saved Egypt from devastation and total ruin. The ravages of famine were becoming more and more acute, until we read, "There was no bread in all the land; for the famine was very sore, so that the land of Egypt and all the land of Canaan fainted by reason of the famine" (Gen. 47:13). When the money failed, then the cattle were given for bread. This provided for another year. At the end of this period, having neither money nor cattle, the people came to Joseph saying, "We will not hide it from my lord, how that our money is spent; my lord also hath our herds of cattle; there is not ought left in the sight of my lord, but our bodies, and our lands: . . . buy us and our land for bread" (47:18, 19). In all this Joseph could not be charged with being unjust or guilty of harsh dealing; indeed you hear the people say to him, "Thou hast saved our lives." You remember the new name Pharaoh gave him, Zaphnath-paaneah, even before preparation for the famine began, the meaning of which was " the saviour of the land." Now its significance is being fully demonstrated, and universally acknowledged.

What a pointer this is, directing us to our Lord Jesus Christ of whom it is said in Hebrews 7:25, "He is able

. . . to save . . . to the uttermost." What a word this is: "able to save to the uttermost"! Many years ago a ship called the *Bywell Castle* had a collision in the river Thames. As a result many were thrown into the water. An old boatman hurried out to pick up those struggling for very life. His boat was soon full to capacity, yet in desperation others clung on, but he could take no more. It is told that he was seen to throw up his arms and cry, "Would God I had a bigger boat!" How willing he was to save, but alas he was not able! Thank God, our Lord Jesus Christ, the Saviour of the world, is not only willing to save, but He is able. He never turns away a needy soul. Did He not say while here on earth, "Him that cometh to Me I will in no wise cast out" (John 6:37)?

What a record we have in the Gospels of His willingness and ability to meet the need of those who came to Him in believing faith. No one was ever turned away. Bless God, though now exalted to heaven's high throne, He is still the same Jesus. Reader, have you ever put Him to the test? Millions in heaven and millions still living on earth have done so, and all testify that He is true to His word and promise, "Him that cometh to Me I will in no wise cast out." Psalm 107:9 declares, "He satisfieth the longing soul, and filleth the hungry soul with goodness."

In contrast to the Egyptians who were tasting the rigors of famine in their own land, Jacob, because of Joseph, was now being provided for in a strange land. Far beyond his expectation he was to be nourished by Joseph for seventeen years. When we remember that back in the vale of Hebron, Jacob had nourished Joseph from the time he was a babe until he was a lad of seventeen years, it would seem as if this was a requital by Joseph for the love and tender care he had been shown in those far-off days.

199

Surely here is a valuable lesson to be learned concerning the duty of children to their parents, especially when advancing years begin to tell their tale. Let son and daughter allow their minds to travel back to those early days, when they were absolutely dependent on their father and mother for everything. What love! what care! what unfailing attention! Is all this to be forgotten? In family life, I can think of nothing grander and nobler than when parents draw near to the sunset of life, to be thus comforted, supported, and generously requited by those who, when unable to provide for themselves in early life, were the recipients of such tender love and care. The blessing for obeying the fifth commandment still stands.

CHAPTER 41

JACOB'S BURIAL INSTRUCTIONS

As Jacob drew near to the termination of life's pilgrimage his burial gets a big place in his thoughts, and as one has said, "Not the pomp of it, but the place of it." He would be buried in Canaan. This he determined, not only because it was the land of his nativity, but more so because it was the land of promise. As Israel, the man of faith, he had firmly grasped the fact, that although that day would be in the far-flung future, it was sure to come according to the covenant promise as the glorious day when God's Israel would people the land from the river Euphrates to the river of Egypt. Jacob never looked upon Egypt as his home, and he wanted to have the assurance before he would die, that his dust would not be left to lie beside the princes of Egypt. To this end he made Joseph sware that he would be buried in the sepulchre of his fathers, Abraham and Isaac, in the land of Canaan.

After blessing his sons in Genesis 49, he charged them, and said unto them, "I am to be gathered unto my people: bury me with my fathers in the cave that is in the field of Ephron the Hittite, in the cave that is in the land of Canaan, which Abraham bought with the field of Ephron the Hittite for a possession of a burying place. There they buried Abraham and Sarah his wife; there they buried Isaac and Rebekah his wife; and there I buried Leah." What an outshining in these words of Israel's inward faith in the covenant-keeping

God! He would be buried in the land of promise, where one day the millions of his seed would find their national home, delivered from all their enemies, and enjoying the peace and tranquility of the great Millennial Day.

These happy seventeen years God granted to the old patriarch were soon to end. There had been no mourning during these years; indeed they were days of uninterrupted happiness. Being near to his loved and long-lost Joseph, and having the promise of God that when the end would come, he would have the one who wore the "coat of many colors," his firstborn by Rachel, to the very last moment, and that he and no other would close for the last time his eyes, this surely was to Jacob the acme of his heart's desire.

In Chapter 48:1 we are told that word was conveyed to Joseph that his father was sick. Knowing that this was a sign that the end was near, he took his two sons, Manasseh and Ephraim, to the bedside of Jacob, and we read, "Israel strengthened himself, and sat upon the bed." These young men, being sons of the lord of the land, might have become princes in Egypt, but Joseph accounted it of much greater importance that they should get the blessing of dying Jacob, and so have a place in his family among the sons of the covenant made with Abraham. To have hands with patriarchal blessing laid upon their heads, would far exceed in kind any honors which Egypt might have conferred upon them. It was that they might obtain such a bless-'ing that Joseph hastened them into his father's presence, for it would have been nothing less than a tragedy to have missed it. "Now the eyes of Israel were dim for age, so that he could not see. And he brought them near unto him; and he kissed them, and embraced them. And Israel said unto Joseph, I had not thought to see thy face: and, lo, God hath showed me also thy seed"

(Gen. 48:10, 11). The joy of the dying patriarch seems to know no bounds, for not only had he been allowed by God to see the face of his long-lost son, but now he is about to lay his hands upon the head of his sons, and bring them into the blessings of the covenant.

Just here I am drawn to think of another dying saint who was full of years. He was found in the temple at Jerusalem when Joseph and Mary went up to present the infant Jesus to the Lord, and to offer a sacrifice according to the law. We read he was "just and devout, waiting for the consolation of Israel: and the Holy Ghost was upon him. And it was revealed unto him by the Holy Ghost, that he should not see death, before he had seen the Lord's Christ." Now when he saw the child Jesus, he took "Him up in his arms, and blessed God, and said, Lord, now lettest Thou Thy servant depart in peace, according to Thy word: for mine eyes have seen Thy salvation, which Thou hast prepared before the face of all people. (See Luke 2: 25-31.)

When it comes to the sunset of life's day, what experience could be more desired than that which Jacob and Simeon had. Both Jacob, as he handed out the blessings of God upon his family, and Simeon, as he held the Lord's Christ in his arms, were most beautifully graced as they stepped out of time into the realm of eternal glory. Reader, whether Christian or not, the day will come when we shall have to leave this world, and enter the next. Does it really give us any serious thought as to how we shall fare in the crossing over? One day an Old Testament monarch, King Saul, approaching that solemn day, had to confess, "I have played the fool, and have erred exceedingly" (1 Sam. 26:21). How different was the verdict, vigor and vision of another man of the same name in the New Testament who could say as he viewed the end of life's road,

"I am now ready to be offered, and the time of my departure is at hand. I have fought a good fight, I have finished my course, I have kept the faith: henceforth there is laid up for me a crown of righteousness, which the Lord, the righteous Judge, shall give me at that day: and not to me only, but unto all them also that love His appearing" (2 Tim. 4:6-8). I have no hesitation in submitting, that for my part, I long to know something of the New Testament Saul's lamentation and regret, when that crisis-day draws near, and the solemn event has to be faced. Let it be remembered, "There is no discharge in that war" (Eccles. 8:8).

CHAPTER 42

THE PATRIARCHAL BLESSING

In relation to the incident of Joseph seeking blessing for his two sons, you may remember that we made mention of this episode in Chapter 1, when dealing with the matter of the firstborn, and the significance of this high honor in patriarchal times. Now we come to deal with the subject in a little more detail.

Joseph's two sons, Manasseh and Ephraim, though born in the land of Egypt, were nevertheless grandsons of Israel, and heirs of the promises made to Abraham, Isaac and Jacob (Israel). Before conferring his blessing on the lads, the old patriarch travels back in memory to the time when God blessed him at Luz (Gen. 28). It was there he was given the covenant promise, when God said to him, "Behold, I will make thee fruitful, and multiply thee, and I will make of thee a multitude of people; and will give this land to thy seed after thee for an everlasting possession." The touching reference he makes to the death of his beloved Rachel (48:3-7) is most significant also, for this links both the lads with the covenant, because their father was his firstborn by Rachel. On this ground he lays claim to both Manasseh and Ephraim saying, "They shall be mine" (48:5).

We pointed out earlier how that in giving the blessing, he did so under direct guidance from God, for in crossing his hands he laid his right hand on the head

205

of Ephraim, the second son, thus giving him the blessing of the firstborn. This was not what Joseph intended, for he had put Manasseh under the right hand of his father, that he might have the firstborn's blessing according to his birth. Seeing the order about to be changed, he protested, but Israel replied, "I know it, my son, I know it: he [Manasseh] also shall become a people, and he also shall be great: but truly his younger brother shall be greater than he, and his seed shall become a multitude of nations. And he blessed them that day, saying, In thee shall Israel bless, saying, God make thee as Ephraim and as Manasseh: and he set Ephraim before Manasseh" (48:19, 20).

In giving the second man the firstborn's blessing, Jacob was following the pattern seen in the divine arrangement when Abraham chose Isaac, and not Ishmael, and when his own father, Isaac, chose him instead of Esau. Likewise as he himself had chosen Joseph instead of Reuben. All this, of course, as we have already pointed out, typified the only One who could be, in one person and at the same time, both the Second Man and the Firstborn. In 1 Corinthians 15:47 we read, "The first man is of the earth, earthy: the second man is the Lord from heaven." Adam was the first man, and Christ was the second man. Psalm 89:27 declares, "Also I will make him my Firstborn, higher than the kings of the earth." He is the One who in all things shall "have the preeminence" (Col. 1:18), or the first place.

Now consider the lesson for the Christian. In Hebrews 12:23 the writer speaks of the Church as "the church of the firstborn ones." This title would appeal to Hebrews. God called Israel his firstborn in relation to earthly blessing, and now He terms the Church, "the assembly of the firstborn ones, which are written in heaven." Romans 8:29 says, "For whom He did foreknow, He also did predestinate to be conformed to the image of His Son, that He might be the first-born among many brethren." Because of the Church's vital union with Christ, the *Firstborn,* who is "the Heir of all things" (Heb. 1:2), she is destined to share with Him the eternal inheritance in the capacity of joint-heirs, while He will ever retain His unique and preeminent place as "the Firstborn among many brethren."

When dealing earlier with the theme of the firstborn, we noted that he had a threefold honor conferred on him, for to him it was given to be the priest and the king of the family, and also the heir to a double portion of the father's inheritance. This again directs us to the Lord Jesus Christ who is the Great High Priest, the King of kings and Heir of all things. Now here is where the practical lesson comes in for the Christian. Since he belongs to the "Church of the firstborn ones," he is called upon to bear a moral likeness to his Lord. In his character and everyday walk the Christian should be marked as a priest by holiness of life (1 Peter 2:5). Being a king, he is called to display the dignified graces associated with the Kingdom of God (Rev. 1:6). Being an heir "to an inheritance incorruptible, and undefiled, and that fadeth not away, reserved in heaven," he must hold loosely the things of this empty world, living and walking as a pilgrim and a stranger until the day when he shall enter into the good of the inheritance, reserved for him in heaven (1 Peter 1:4 and 2:11). Paul's word in Ephesians 4:1 would be appropriate here for every disciple of Christ: "Walk worthy of the vocation wherewith ye are called."

In blessing the lads, Israel travels back into the past in sacred memory to the association of his fathers, Abraham and Isaac, with the God of the covenant, and how they had walked before Him. He next recalls the

207

faithfulness of that same Covenant-God, saying, "The God which fed me all my life long unto this day." Thirdly, "The Angel which redeemed me from all evil, bless the lads" (Gen. 48:15, 16). What a weight of evidence Israel had, giving him confidence and assurance, that the God to whom he was about to commend the lads, was the faithful, covenant-keeping God, whose words cannot be broken, and whose promises never fail. I would have you notice the mention he made of "The Angel which redeemed me from all evil." He was not referring to one of the angelic host, but to the second Person of the Holy Trinity, the pre-incarnate Christ. This is clearly seen at Peniel (Gen. 32:30), and is also confirmed by the prophet Hosea who, when speaking of Jacob's experience at Peniel, says, "Yea, he had power over the Angel, and prevailed: he wept, and made supplication unto him: he found him in Bethel, and there he spake with us; even *the Lord God of hosts; the Lord is his memorial"* (Hosea 12:4, 5). Jacob could well join with the patriarch Job and say, "I know that my Redeemer liveth" (Job 19:25).

To deal with this great title of our Lord Jesus Christ, Redeemer, and the prominence it has in the Holy Scriptures, would take us outside the bounds of this present work. All I would say is, let the reader take a long look at Calvary, for it was there, transfixed to a Roman cross, He went into action as the Redeemer of men. The New Testament word "redemption" is brimful of meaning. It conveys the thought of one stepping into the slave market to pay the ransom price demanded for the release of the captive slave, a price that would not only lift him out of the market, but bring him into glorious liberty, never to be in the slave market again. In a spiritual sense that is what the Redeemer has done for every one who rests on Calvary's finished work. He has lifted them out of the bondage of sin's slavery, and from the domination of Satan, no more to be led captive by him at his will. Referring to such a deliverance the Saviour said in John 8:36, "If the Son therefore shall make you free, ye shall be free indeed."

D. W. Whittle wrote:

Come, sing, my soul, and praise the Lord,
Who hath redeemed thee by His blood;
Delivered thee from chains that bound,
And brought thee to redemption ground.
Oh, joyous hour when God to me
A vision gave of Calvary:
My bonds were loosed, my soul unbound;
I sang upon redemption ground.

CHAPTER 43

ISRAEL, BLESSER AND PROPHET

The dying Israel, in blessing Ephraim and Manasseh, blessed Joseph (Gen. 48:15), giving him the double portion which was his right being the firstborn of Israel by Rachel. At a later day, when Joshua was dividing the Promised Land by lot so that each tribe would have its own inheritance, Joseph had a double portion, for two large stretches of territory were given for possession to his two sons with their tribes. Having blessed the lads, the old patriarch said unto Joseph, "Behold, I die: but God shall be with you, and bring you again unto the land of your fathers" (48:21). How firmly he grasped the covenant promise that his seed should inherit the land of his fathers Abraham and Isaac! He recognized that it was in the plan of God that in Egypt his seed should become a great nation; but eventually they would leave it forever and find their national home in the God-given Promised Land.

Today, in the year 1973, Israel is back in her own land, and though not yet in full possession, she has, with full national status, become fabulously wealthy. In this we see the Word of God having its fulfillment, and it shows that the time is near when the divine promise will be carried out to the full and the land will be possessed from the river Euphrates to the Nile. What a day of glory that will be, when the scattered of Israel shall be gathered home, and Jerusalem becomes the joy of the whole earth, with the Lord Jesus

Christ, their true Messiah, sitting as David's royal Son, on David's royal throne!

Chapter 49 opens with Israel calling his sons together. "Gather yourselves together, that I may tell you that which shall befall you in the last days. Gather yourselves together, and hear, ye sons of Jacob; and hearken unto Israel your father" (vv. 1, 2). The words which he was about to speak were uttered as prophecy, mingled with blessing. As he was in the last hour of his life, these words to his sons are his final words. Can we think of a more solemn occasion in any family? Those who have been called to stand at the bedside of a dying loved one, straining the ear for every last word, can truly picture the scene now before us. The interview lasted no longer than ten minutes. His word to each tribe was short; the longest was his word to Joseph, yet that took only about twenty seconds. Judah's word came next, occupying only eight seconds, yet every word was exceedingly weighty being uttered by divine inspiration. The expression Israel uses on this occasion "the last days," is of great significance. The Jewish rabbis always took this to mean the Messianic era and is equivalent to the "end time" of Daniel 12:9. The expositor F. Delitzsch defines it as "denoting not the future course of history that forms the present, but the future which forms the close of history." It is the day Isaiah speaks of when Christ the Messiah in the midst of Israel will also be the center of light and peace to the nations of the world. "And it shall come to pass in the last days, that the mountain of the Lord's house shall be established in the top of the mountains, and shall be exalted above the hills; and all nations shall flow unto it" (Isa. 2:2-4). Hosea refers to the time yet future, when Israel will have been punished severely for their unbelief and for their rejection and crucifixion of their Messiah, after which the day of reconciliation

211

will come. He says, "Afterward shall the children of Israel return, and seek the Lord their God, and David their king; and shall fear the Lord . . . in the latter days" (Hosea 3:5).

My reason for introducing you to this important chapter (49) is not only because the great prophecy it contains is the key to the Scripture account of Israel's twelve tribes whose history finds a place in the whole of sacred Scripture from Genesis to Revelation, but it is that we might look at the word of the father to his beloved Joseph, upon whose shoulders one day long ago, he laid the "coat of many colors," the coat that had altered the whole course of history for father and son. Indeed the story that has occupied our attention thus far, from the time of Joseph's experience at Dothan, when that coat was torn from him, and dipped in blood to deceive the old father, never could have been told apart from that happening. That was the basic incident upon which the drama of the past forty years rested.

CHAPTER **44**

A FATHER'S BLESSING TO JOSEPH

Jacob's blessing for Joseph is found in Genesis 49:
22-26. The father begins by saying, "Joseph is a fruitful bough, even a fruitful bough by a well; whose
branches run over the wall." This poetical description
presents a beautiful picture of fruitfulness and fertility.
The word "bough" in the original Hebrew Scriptures
is *ben* meaning "son"; for "branches," *banoth,* meaning "daughters." The words "son" and "branch" are
sometimes interchanged, for as the branch is part of
the tree and partakes of its life, nature and strength,
so the son is the offspring of the father. We think then
of the son of a tree as equivalent to a branch.

Here we are introduced to one of the many significant titles of our Lord Jesus Christ, Israel's Messiah—
the "Branch." In Isaiah 11:1 we read, "There shall
come forth a rod out of the stem of Jesse, and a Branch
shall grow out of his roots." Again the prophet says,
speaking of the great millennial day yet future, "In
that day shall the branch of the Lord be beautiful and
glorious" (Isa. 4:2). From this we learn that as to
His manhood, He is figuratively described as the Branch
or Sprout of David, and as to His Godhead He is the
Branch of Jehovah. This is the One of whom Paul
spoke in 1 Timothy 3:16 when he said, "Great is the
mystery of godliness: *God* was manifest in the *flesh.*"

One day while here on earth the Saviour claimed to
be David's Lord, and at the same time to be David's

213

Son. Indeed, before the book of the Revelation closes He says to John, "I *Jesus* have sent Mine angel to testify unto you these things in the churches. I am the *root* and the *offspring* of David, and the bright and morning star" (22:16). The poet, looking at these two natures—*divine* and *human*—so perfectly blended in the Person of the Lord Jesus Christ, put it beautifully when he wrote:

> *Of God the best expression,*
> *Of man the finest specimen,*
> *Full-orbed humanity,*
> *Crowned with Deity!*

> *Ecce Homo — Behold the* MAN,
> *Ecce Deus — Behold thy* GOD!
> *Veiled in flesh, the Godhead see,*
> *Hail — Incarnate Deity!*

Israel not only spoke of Joseph as a bough, but as a "fruitful bough." This was no doubt because he was the father of Ephraim and Manasseh, whose tribes would be a multitude. At the end of their wilderness journey, these were the largest of all the tribes, having 85,200 men of twenty years old and upward. Linked with the thought of "productiveness" is his "place" by a well. The well is the source of his fruitfulness. "His branches run over the wall" refer to his people, who would become so prolific, that Israel could speak of the ten thousands of Ephraim and the thousands of Manasseh. This description of Joseph is Messianic in character. First, as the "fruitful bough," we saw the original word for "bough" was equal to "son," so we view the Lord Jesus Christ as the "Son" — Son of God, Son of Man, Son of the Father, the Eternal Son. As such He is inscrutable as to His Person, "No man knoweth the Son but the Father."

> *True image of the Infinite,*
> *Whose essence is concealed,*
> *Brightness of uncreated light,*
> *The heart of God revealed.*

Considering our Lord as the "fruitful bough" we see Him in the perfection of His work. In John 12:24 His own words were, "Verily, verily, I say unto you, Except a corn of wheat fall into the ground and die, it abideth alone: but if it die, it bringeth forth much fruit." Another has said, "How plain it is that this is no accidental likeness which the Lord here seizes for illustration of His point. It is as real a prediction as ever came from the lips of an Old Testament prophet; every seed sown in the ground, to produce a harvest, is a positive prediction that the Giver of life must die." On Calvary Christ dies. He dies alone.

> *Alone upon the cross He hung,*
> *That others He might save;*
> *Forsaken then, by God Himself,*
> *Alone His life He gave.*

One day in the temple, when challenged as to His power and authority, He answered, "Destroy this temple, and in three days I will raise it up." Then said the Jews, "Forty and six years was this temple in building, and wilt Thou rear it up in three days?" But He spake of the temple of His body (John 2:19-21). We leave the tree, and visit the tomb; the three days have passed of which He spoke, and what do we find? A heavenly messenger is there to greet us with these triumphant words, "He is not here: He is risen, as He said. Come, see the place where the Lord lay" (Matt. 28:6).

> *Vain the stone, the watch, the seal,*
> *Christ has burst the gates of hell;*
> *Vain their efforts to enthrall,*
> *He has triumphed over all.*

215

Christ our Lord is risen indeed,
Christ is now the Church's head;
Loud the song of triumph raise,
Celebrate the Victor's praise.

It is in His resurrection we see the answer to the "fruitful bough." Paul in 1 Corinthians 15:19-22 says, "If in this life only we have hope in Christ, we are of all men most miserable. But now is Christ risen from the dead, and become the firstfruits of them that slept. For since by man came death, by man came also the resurrection of the dead. For as in Adam all die, even so in Christ shall all be made alive." Colossians 1:18 reads, "And He is the head of the body, the church: who is the beginning, the firstborn from the dead; that in all things He might have the preeminence." The expression "Christ . . . the firstfruits" calls us back in mind to Leviticus 23:9-14 where we have the third of Israel's annual festivals, called the Feast of Firstfruits. There Jehovah commands the nation, saying, "When ye be come into the land which I give unto you, and shall reap the harvest thereof, then ye shall bring a sheaf of the firstfruits of your harvest unto the priest: and he shall wave the sheaf before the Lord, to be accepted for you: on the morrow after the sabbath the priest shall wave it."

Notice the word, "On the morrow after the sabbath." No specific date is ever given for this ceremony; it is always, "The morrow after the sabbath" (vv. 10, 11). Here surely is the link with Matthew 28:1, 2: "In the end of the sabbath, as it began to dawn toward the first day of the week, came Mary Magdalene and the other Mary to see the sepulchre. And, behold, there was a great earthquake: for the angel of the Lord descended from heaven, and came and rolled back the stone from the door, and sat upon it." Out from the great realm of the dead, He came as the Firstfruits, the

Antitype of the "first wave sheaf" (Lev. 23:9-14).
The Lord Jesus in Colossians 1:18 is seen as "Firstborn from among the dead ones." When Israel was in
Canaan, and the time of the barley harvest arrived, it
was then the priest of old lifted the "first sheaf" out of
the field. This sheaf was the first of the golden harvest,
the remainder of which would follow in due course.
It told that the day of resurrection glory had arrived.
This is surely the divine order as seen in 1 Corinthians
15:22, 23: "For as in Adam all die, even so in Christ
shall all be made alive. But every man in his own
order: Christ the *Firstfruits;* afterward they that are
Christ's at His coming."

The Christian looks forward to that great day of in-
gathering, at the coming of the Lord for His Church.
At the sound of His voice and the blast of the trumpet,
every grave will yield up its dead; bodies which lie in
the ocean's depths will obey the divine summons. Paul
says, "The dead in Christ shall rise first." "This corruptible must put on incorruption." The cry of glorified
saints in that day will be, "O death, where is thy sting?
O grave, where is thy victory?" Christ rising from the
dead is the "first wave sheaf." The resurrection and
glorification of the Church will be the gathering in of
the great harvest of which He was the "firstfruits."

Passing from the thought of Joseph's productivity,
as the "fruitful bough," let us move on to consider the
place — "by a well." This was the secret of its fruitfulness; it drew its sap from the hidden depths. Does
this not speak to us in New Testament language of the
gracious supply of the indwelling Holy Spirit? John
3:34 speaks of our Lord Jesus Christ, the Heavenly
Joseph. There it says, "God giveth not the Spirit by
measure unto Him." He was conceived in the Spirit,
He was anointed by the Spirit, He wrought miracles by
the power of the Spirit, He was led by the Spirit, He

217

offered Himself without spot to God, through the Eternal Spirit, He was declared to be the Son of God with power according to the Spirit of holiness by the resurrection of the dead. It is the same Holy Spirit that seals and indwells the Christian (Eph. 1:13; Rom. 8:11). In John 7:38, 39, Jesus said, " 'He that believeth on Me, as the scripture hath said, out of his belly shall flow rivers of living water.' (. . . this spake He of the Spirit . . .)" To the woman of Samaria, Jesus said, "Whosoever drinketh of the water that I shall give him shall never thirst; but the water that I shall give him shall be in him a well of water springing up into everlasting life" (John 4:14). This is the power that is at the disposal of every Christian. It is this power operating within, that makes him more than conqueror. It is by allowing Him to take control of the life that the fruit of the Spirit is produced—"love, joy, peace, longsuffering, gentleness, goodness, faith, meekness, self-control" (Gal. 5:22, 23).

All these were fully displayed in the life of the Lord Jesus Christ, and they will be seen in the life of the Christian whose mind and movements are regulated and directed by the Holy Spirit of God. How necessary is the command of Ephesians 4:30, "Grieve not the Holy Spirit of God, whereby ye are sealed unto the day of redemption." The previous verses of this chapter show the many ways by which Christians may grieve the Holy Spirit. We must keep our lives clean by the sanctifying power of the Word of God, applying it to our daily conduct, our thoughts, our words, and our ways. We remember the Lord's prayer for His own, "Sanctify them through Thy truth: Thy word is truth" (John 17:17). Psalm 119:9 asks, "Wherewithal shall a young man cleanse his way? [and answers] by taking heed thereto according to Thy word." How necessary it is that we take heed to the exhortation given in Ephesians

4:22-32, so as not to fall into any of those damaging sins that grieve the Holy Spirit, for if this happens, we lose the sense of God's presence, and are shorn of the power to produce the fruit of the Spirit in our daily lives.

What did old Israel mean when he spoke of Joseph as the fruitful bough "whose branches run over the wall"? As I remarked earlier, it would seem to be in connection with the spread of his descendants, for in later days when the tribes received their inheritance in Canaan, we find Manasseh with territory on either side of Jordan. Ephraim's inheritance was large and planted in a very pleasant place. It would appear that Joseph's posterity was to be so fruitful as to overstep the bounds of the inheritance originally intended for them. By this prophetic statement, are we not again directed to our Lord Jesus Christ, who in His fruitfulness became the Saviour for all men who would believe? His branches went over the wall of Judaism, and spread out into the nations of the Gentiles. They passed over the tremendous barrier that stood between God and man. Such walls and barriers were removed by His atoning death on Calvary, so that they who were afar off could be made nigh. Indeed, that is how Paul put it to the Gentile church at Ephesus: "But now in Christ Jesus ye who sometimes were far off are made nigh by the blood of Christ" (2:13).

CHAPTER 45

THE BLESSING FOR JOSEPH

After speaking of Joseph's posterity, old Jacob now looks back over Joseph's history, and says, "The archers have sorely grieved him, and shot at him, and hated him: but his bow abode in strength, and the arms of his hands were made strong by the hands of the mighty God of Jacob" (49:23, 24). No doubt he was traveling back in mind to those early days, when Joseph was so ill-treated by his brethren, when they envied him, hated him, and could not speak peaceably unto him. They were the cruel archers who shot at him. Their treatment of him at Dothan was no longer a secret. Israel, now fully acquainted with the happenings of that day, in thought saw poor Joseph sorely wounded, robbed of his "coat of many colors" and handed over to years of slavery. We know, too, how that wicked woman shot her arrows at him; for her own sinful pleasure, she would rob him of his character, and put a blemish on his life that would remain to the end of his days.

This was followed by further wounding when his master had him cast into the dungeon and condemned as a criminal. How hard this was to bear, for one who was absolutely innocent! Despite all this, Israel goes on to say in a voice of triumph, "But his bow abode in strength." This simply means he endured all this affliction and emerged at the end, undefeated and victorious, and this because "the arms of his hands were made strong by the hands of the mighty God of Jacob." During those times we read again and again, "The Lord was with Joseph." This was the secret of his overcoming in the fight to maintain his integrity, and of his leaving the contest without a single scar.

The Christian could learn a lesson here. Every one who names the name of Christ and owns Him as Lord, finds that the Christian life is a warfare. Daily he is assailed by an inveterate and cruel foe, threefold in character — the world, the flesh, and the devil. Any one of them is more than a match for the Christian. Should he attempt to meet the enemy in his own strength, the result would be defeat. One day the world got the better of Demas (2 Tim. 4:10). The flesh bowled over the offender at Corinth (1 Cor. 5:4, 5). Poor Peter; Satan desired him "that he might sift him as wheat," and when the test came, Peter lost his courage and denied his Lord (Luke 22:31). It is good to know he never lost his faith. Of course, the reason for that was, the Saviour had said to Peter, "I have prayed for thee, that thy faith fail not" (Luke 22:32).

How necessary it is, then, that we so live, as to know and appreciate the Lord's help and presence in daily experience for it is only in this way that we can meet the enemy, ward off his attacks, and continue to be "more than conquerors through Him that loved us" (Rom. 8:37). How beautifully Paul illustrates this in his own experience when he was being tried for his life before Nero. He said to Timothy, "At my first answer no man stood with me, but all men forsook me. . . . Notwithstanding the *Lord stood with me,* and strengthened me" (2 Tim. 4:16, 17). In Exodus 32:11-14 we find Moses crying to the Lord, when in the midst of that stiffnecked people who brought down Jehovah's judgment upon them for worshiping the golden calf; he cried for mercy on the ground of the covenant made with Abraham. The wilderness journey lay ahead with all its trials and difficulties and how could Moses face up to it with such a gainsaying and rebellious people?

221

The Lord heard his earnest cry and responded with, "My presence shall go with thee, and I will give thee rest." Note Moses' reply: "If Thy presence go not with me, carry us not up hence" (Exod. 33:14, 15). To him the accompanying presence of God was indispensable, and so it is with the Christian.

Genesis 49:24 brings us to a very important, yet difficult statement: "From thence is the shepherd, the stone of Israel." May I suggest that "from thence" could mean "from these things," that is to say, from Joseph's fruitfulness, from his grief and sorrow, from the hatred he experienced, from his strengthening by the "hand of the mighty God of Jacob"; from these things we may derive a foreshadowing of the Heavenly Joseph, Christ Himself, who was the Shepherd and Stone of Israel. There is no doubt as to the fact that as far as Jacob and his family were concerned, Joseph could be looked upon as their shepherd; how he cared for them, how he tended them, and how he fed them in the day of famine! Again, as "the stone" he was the foundation upon which they rested in the land of Goshen; it was for Joseph's sake Pharaoh so richly blessed them, but as I have said, Joseph is but a type of the Lord Jesus Christ, the Good Shepherd (John 10:11), the Great Shepherd (Heb. 13:20), and the Chief Shepherd (1 Pet. 5:4), of the New Testament.

You see, we have to remember that in verse 10 of our chapter, we read, "The sceptre shall not depart from Judah, nor a lawgiver from between his feet, until Shiloh come; and unto him shall the gathering of the people be." Hebrews 7:14, as mentioned before, emphasizes this point saying, "It is evident that our Lord sprang out of Judah." (Of course, this is connected with His Royal Priesthood.) In Ephesians 2:20 the Lord Jesus Christ is seen as the Chief Corner Stone, upon which the Church rests. He is her sure foundation. I wonder if the reader can say in truth, "The Lord is my Shepherd," and knows what it is to rest upon Christ the *Stone,* "for other foundation can no man lay" (1 Cor. 3:11).

Proceeding with his blessing, Israel predicts that Joseph shall have the help of the God of his father, the Almighty God, blessing him with the blessings of heaven above, blessings of the deep that lieth under, blessings of the breasts, and of the womb. He uses the idea of infinite distance, "heaven above," and plumbs the hidden deep, to describe the immensity and the boundlessness of God's blessing that lay in the future for Joseph's posterity. The "blessing of the breasts and of the womb" had to do with the prolific increase in the nation's population, built up through the tribes of Ephraim and Manasseh, of which these two sons of Joseph were the heads.

The title Israel uses for the God who would command the blessing, is most precious—"The Almighty." It means "the all-sufficient One." This is consistent with the covenant blessing, for Genesis 17:1-8 shows that this is how God appeared to Abram. We read there, "And when Abram was ninety years old and nine, the Lord appeared to Abram, and said unto him, I am the *Almighty God;* walk before Me, and be thou perfect. And I will make My *covenant* between Me and thee, and will multiply thee exceedingly. And Abram fell on his face: and God talked with him, saying, As for Me, behold, My covenant is with thee, and thou shalt be a father of many nations. Neither shall thy name any more be called Abram, but thy name shall be Abraham; for a father of many nations have I made thee. And I will make thee exceeding fruitful, and I will make nations of thee, and kings shall come out of thee. And I will establish My covenant between Me and thee and thy seed after thee in their generations

223

for an everlasting covenant, to be a God unto thee, and to thy seed after thee. And I will give unto thee, and to thy seed after thee, the land wherein thou art a stranger, all the land of Canaan, for an everlasting possession."

I have quoted these verses in full just to let the reader see how the old patriarch, Israel, was in line with the mind and purpose of God in blessing Joseph, in the name of *The Almighty God,* the God of the *covenant.* Continuing at verse 26, Israel, when dying, claims to be happier than even Abraham or Isaac. It is true, that in speaking to Pharaoh, when asked how old he was, he replied, "Few and evil have the days of the years of my life been, and have not attained unto the days of the years of the life of my fathers in the days of their pilgrimage." He undoubtedly had known more of trouble and affliction than either Abraham or his own father Isaac, and, of course, had fewer years allotted to him than they had. Why then does he use the word progenitors (Gen. 49:26) of Abraham and Isaac? I believe he looked upon himself as much inferior to Abraham as far as spiritual endowments went, neither would he place himself alongside Isaac. In saying what he said, he acknowledged the sovereign goodness of God.

When his progenitors gave their blessing, things were different; Abraham had a blessing for Isaac, Jacob could recall that it was on his head alone Isaac laid his hands, as he gave him the covenant blessing. Now twelve sons, for whom he has blessing, are gathered round his bed, and not one of them is left out or denied. True, he had hard things to say betimes, and here and there administered reproofs, but rising above all this, was the fact that to every one of them was given the glorious hope of a share in the land of promise. Israel's concluding words in the blessing of Joseph are, "The blessings of thy father have prevailed above the blessings of my progenitors unto the utmost bound of the everlasting hills: they shall be on the head of Joseph, and on the crown of the head of him that was separate from his brethren" (Gen. 49:26).

"Unto the utmost bound of the everlasting hills" is an expression, the meaning of which is a little difficult to ascertain. I rather like the way the scholarly Edersheim puts it (*World Before the Flood*: footnote, page 186): "That is, as far as the mountains overtop the plains, so the blessings which Joseph now receives, exceed those which any of Jacob's ancestors had bestowed." Others see these blessings, stretching far beyond time into the unending days of eternity, thus making them endless as to their duration. Again, there are those who view the hills as places where the patriarchs sometimes presented their sacrifices to God, one of them in particular being the holy hill of Zion where the Lord had been pleased to place His name, and which He promised to establish forever. Psalm 133 says, "There the Lord commanded the blessing, even life for evermore." Lawson says, "When the Psalmist directed the views of the people to the hills from whence came their help, he certainly did not mean that their salvation was to be expected from the hills, or from the multitude of mountains, but from the Lord who dwelt in Zion" (*History of Joseph*, page 544). This view seems to be corroborated by Psalm 87:1-3: "His foundation is in the holy mountains. The Lord loveth the gates of Zion more than all the dwellings of Jacob. Glorious things are spoken of thee, O city of God. Selah."

CHAPTER 46

JACOB'S LAST WORDS TO JOSEPH

We will now consider the very last utterance of Israel's copious blessing conferred upon his loved, and long-lost son Joseph. Referring to every item that was included in the blessing, he said, "They shall be on the head of Joseph, and on the crown of the head of him that was separate from his brethren" (Gen. 49:26). What a word this is: "separate from his brethren"! Here Joseph's history is crammed into four words. How separate he was in his childhood! Do you remember when Jacob his father went in fear and trembling to meet Esau, and how he put in the forefront the other sons, but brought on Rachel, the mother, and her six-year-old Joseph hindermost?

Later, at the age of seventeen, his father honored him with the "coat of many colors" as the firstborn, priest of the family, and how this marked him out as separate from his brethren who wore the rough garb of the shepherd. His daily life and conduct, too, were of such a character that it was plainly seen by Jacob, that indeed Joseph was separate from his brethren. When he was with his brethren looking after the flock we read, "He brought unto his father their evil report." This reveals the difference between their conduct and his. How separate he was from them in relation to his God-given dreams! We never read of any of his brethren having communications from heaven. When Jacob in his blessing said earlier, "The archers sorely grieved him, and shot at him, and hated him," he was going back in mind to these days when Joseph, the God-fearing lad, stood out separate from them, as the object of their envy and bitter hatred. Then followed the crisis at Dothan when he was forcibly and physically made to be separate from his brethren, a separation that was to last for twenty years, and what a twenty years that was for Joseph! Though innocent, he was charged as guilty; he was condemned unjustly, put in the dungeon, and numbered with the transgressors.

Then came the day of exaltation, when Joseph became lord of Egypt and saviour of the land—from the lowest place he has mounted to the highest place. What a pen-picture of him who was separate from his brethren, when we look at them coming in before him, as he sat in all the pomp and state, suited to his elevated position as next to Pharaoh. See them also at a later day lying before him with their faces to the ground, and calling him "my lord." For years to come, we also see Joseph in his exalted station, caring for them in the land of Goshen, as a good shepherd would care for his sheep. Indeed he was their saviour in the day of grievous famine, and provided for them a home in the rich pastures of Goshen. How truly he was separate from his brethren!

In dealing with these outstanding instances where we see Joseph separate from his brethren, we cannot but see him, in this sense, as an outstanding type of our Lord Jesus Christ. How separate He was in His childhood from His Israelitish brethren! See Him as a lad of twelve among the doctors in the temple, "both hearing them and answering their questions." Again, as He entered His public ministry which began with His baptism, we read in Matthew that "Jesus, when He was baptized, went up straightway out of the

227

water: and, lo, the heavens were opened unto Him, and He saw the Spirit of God descending like a dove, and lighting upon Him: and lo a voice from heaven, saying, This is My beloved Son, in whom I am well pleased" (3:16, 17). Here again we see, that although many were baptized that day, Jesus stood out separate from them all, as the Father's beloved Son. In the three and a half years which followed, that separation became more and more apparent because of His consecrated life, and His deep-toned devotion to the will of His Father God. Like Joseph, being thus distinguished as the Beloved Son, caused Him to become the object of cruel hatred. That holy, sinless life that He lived was an open condemnation to the hypocritical and godless manner of living that marked the nation in His day. How separate He was even from His own brethren; John 7:5 says, "Neither did His brethren believe in Him."

So bitter was the hatred of the religious leaders, that they dogged His steps, trying to catch Him in His words that they might accuse Him. Indeed, they never rested until they had Him brought to trial, and finally nailed to Golgotha's tree. Joseph's brethren hated him and engineered the plan to get rid of him: they stripped him of his "coat of many colors," and cast him into the pit, and handed him over to the Ishmeelites for the price of a slave. All this surely foreshadows the treatment meted out to the Lord Jesus by His own brethren according to the flesh. "He came unto His own and His own received Him not." They hated Him, and rejected Him; He was betrayed and handed over to the enemy for the price of a slave, He was stripped of His raiment, He was made to cry, "I sink in the deep mire, where there is no standing." His wicked tormentors could not be satisfied until they had Him "cut off out of the land of the living."

Joseph in Egypt, innocently condemned, cast into the dungeon where the iron entered his soul, cut off from the outside world for 20 long years, faintly pictures our "Heavenly Joseph." Pilate said, "I find no fault in Him." Christ Himself could say, "They hated Me without a cause." Yet to the depths of Calvary He went, to experience that awful separation, when He was forsaken by God and man. It is here the type fails, for Joseph, during those lonely years, suffered much, yet he was never forsaken by his God. But Christ was! Hear that heart-rending cry from the center tree, "My God, My God, why hast Thou forsaken Me?" (Matt. 27: 46). It tells us that the sufferings of our Lord Jesus Christ were *atoning* sufferings. Isaiah 53:5 and 6 declares why He so suffered. "He was wounded for our transgressions, He was bruised for our iniquities: the chastisement of our peace was upon Him; and with His stripes we are healed. All we like sheep have gone astray; we have turned every one to his own way; and the Lord hath laid on Him the iniquity of us all."

> *He took the guilty sinner's place,*
> *And suffered in His stead,*
> *For man, O miracle of grace,*
> *For man the Saviour bled.*

By faith every Christian prostrates himself before Calvary's bleeding Victim and confesses, "I am the guilty sinner, but Jesus died for me."

When Joseph's brethren got rid of him that day at Dothan they never expected to see him again. The object of their hatred and envy was gone. Now they could live in peace and forget him. But could they do so? True, they had put him in the lowest place, for he went down to the pavement of the dungeon, but little did they know, that this was the road to his God-given ex-

229

altation and to his rising to ride in the second chariot of Pharaoh, while the thousands of Egypt were commanded to bow the knee before him, as the lord of Egypt, and the saviour of the land. It never dawned on them either that the day would come when they themselves would bow the knee before him, lick the dust in his presence, and gladly take the place of servants, and that Judah himself one day for Benjamin's sake would offer to be Joseph's willing slave. Yet that day did come, causing them the deepest humiliation and confusion of face, as we have already seen.

What a pointer this is to the case of our Lord Jesus Christ! His murderers were sure they had gotten rid of Him, for when the darkness lifted at Calvary they could see His pale and bloodless body, the unmistakable evidence that Jesus of Nazareth was dead. They would have said, "That is the end of Him; we will see now what will become of His claims." No doubt at Dothan the brethren said the same, relative to Joseph's dreams. The hands of those who loved Jesus laid His dead body in the tomb. But was this the end? There were those among His enemies who were inwardly troubled, knowing He had said that He would rise again. So by Pilate's command they sealed the stone and ordered a guard, but at the divinely appointed moment, God exerted the strength of His might, and up from the grave Christ arose.

The words He spoke to His enemies in John 2:19 were now fulfilled: "Destroy this temple [His body], and in three days I will raise it up." He exercises His own inherent power, by which He vanquished the powers of hell and darkness. He "abolished death, and hath brought life and immortality to light through the gospel" (2 Tim. 1:10). Upon this great fact rests the whole fabric of the Christian faith. It is no wonder that from the day the tomb was emptied, until this very day,

Satan amassed all his emissaries to attack it, and deny
it. If the brethren of Joseph were brought down in
utter confusion at the reappearing, and manifestation of
his glory, how will that unnumbered mass of Christ-
rejecting sinners feel? What consternation will be theirs
when at the final assize they behold the Judge, "from
whose face the earth and the heaven fled away" (Rev.
20:11)! It is as the glorified Man of Calvary that they
shall see Him, for the assurance that God hath given to
all men that it shall be so, is this—"He has raised Him
from the dead" (Acts 17:31).

We will now consider the very last favor of the dying
father conferred on his loved son Joseph. "And Israel
said unto Joseph, Behold, I die: but God shall be with
you, and bring you again unto the land of your fathers.
Moreover I have given to thee one portion above thy
brethren, which I took out of the hand of the Amorite
with my sword and with my bow" (Gen. 48:21, 22).
"I die: but God shall be with you." It was as if he
said, Your father is dying, but the God of Abraham,
Isaac and Jacob will not die; He will be with you; the
Covenant-keeping God lives on.

What a comfort these words would be to Joseph!
Following this, Israel projects his mind to the fulfillment of the covenant promise in relation to the land
of Palestine, which God first gave to Abraham, then
passed on to Isaac, and at Luz was given to himself;
for he declares that the God who will be with him will
bring him again into the land of his fathers (v. 21).
This, of course, referred to Joseph's posterity.

Israel now ends with a special favor for Joseph,
"Moreover I have given thee one portion above thy
brethren." In that day long ago at Shechem he showed
his favor to Joseph in robing him with the "coat of
many colors"; now with his dying breath he again would
identify him as his beloved son, by giving him an ex-

231

clusive portion of the land as his very own, and what should it be but Shechem, the place of hallowed memory. This was the portion of land, that he bought from the men of Shechem for a hundred pieces of silver (Gen. 33:19). As to the next statement he made, "Which I took out of the hand of the Amorite with my sword and with my bow," we have no information. It is possible that when he left Shechem for the time being, the Amorites took possession of it, and that later Jacob by divine direction with his armed servants drove them out, for, after all, it was his by right of purchase. It is impossible to leave these thoughts without referring to John 4:5 where we read that when Jesus was passing through Samaria He came to a "city . . . called Sychar, near to the parcel of ground that Jacob gave to his son Joseph."

After the death of Jacob that land would be for many years occupied by the people of Canaan, but the day did come when Israel entered that land under Joshua. The posterity of Joseph would place a high value upon it, because it had been given to the father of the tribe in promise, from Israel's death-bed. It is wonderful to see in John 4, as Jesus sat on the well at Sychar, how the Samaritan woman confirmed the God-given record of Genesis 48:22, saying to Jesus, "Art thou greater than our father Jacob, which gave us the well, and drank thereof himself, and his children, and his cattle?" (v. 12). It is surely touching to think that the very spot that Jacob gave to his loved son, should provide a resting place for Heaven's Firstborn, God's beloved Son, the Lord of glory.

CHAPTER 47

JACOB'S FINAL CHARGE

Israel's final charge to his twelve sons is recorded in Genesis 49:29-32: "He charged them, and said unto them, I am to be gathered unto my people: bury me with my fathers in the cave that is in the field of Ephron the Hittite, in the cave that is in the field of Machpelah, which is before Mamre, in the land of Canaan, which Abraham bought with the field of Ephron the Hittite for the possession of a burying place. There they buried Abraham and Sarah his wife; there they buried Isaac and Rebekah his wife; and there I buried Leah. The purchase of the field and of the cave that is therein was from the children of Heth."

The seventeen years in the land of Egypt near to Joseph were precious years to the aged patriarch, and no doubt, being in favor with Pharaoh, he might have had, if he had so wished, a funeral with royal honors, on account of being the father of Joseph, the governor of Egypt. His dying charge to the brethren left them in no doubt as to the place of his burial. By divine direction he had been guided to Egypt. There, because of Joseph, he and all he had, had been abundantly provided for in the years of famine, and he knew God would fulfill His promise to make Israel a great nation. Yet, despite all this, in his dying moments the place that filled his vision was the land of his fathers, and that sacred plot where lay their remains, the cave in the field of Machpelah. Die in Egypt he must; but Machpelah in the land of Canaan would be the resting place for his bones. The name of this patriarchal cemetery is most suggestive as to its meaning. It means "the way in and the way out." Does it embrace the thought of resurrection? I submit it does. There was a way into the new tomb of Joseph of Arimathea for the body of the Saviour, but the third day showed there was a way out. So it will be for the blessed dead who lie in their graves, for in speaking about the coming of the Lord Jesus Christ to rapture the Church to eternal glory, Paul says, "the dead in Christ shall rise first" (1 Thess. 4:16). That will be "the way out." The victor's cry of that day will be, "O death, where is thy sting? O grave, where is thy victory? . . . Thanks be to God, who giveth us the victory through our Lord Jesus Christ" (1 Cor. 15:55-57).

Reader, as you look forward to the grave and its beyond ("for we must needs die," 2 Sam. 14:14), have you the blessed assurance that you will share in the glorious resurrection to eternal life? If not, accept a kindly warning, for those who share not in this resurrection of the just, will be left to share the resurrection of the unjust in the day of God's wrath and judgment (Rev. 20:11-15). Israel's determination to be buried in Machpelah, shows him as the man of faith, resting in sweetest peace, and implicitly relying on the fulfillment of the covenant promise. Hebrews 11:21 reads, "By faith Jacob, when he was a dying, blessed both the sons of Joseph; and worshipped, leaning upon the top of his staff." After Israel had blessed his sons, and given charge concerning his burial, Genesis 49:33 says, "He gathered up his feet into the bed, and yielded up the ghost, and was gathered unto his fathers."

Genesis 50 opens thus: "And Joseph fell upon his father's face and wept upon him, and kissed him." Such partings are never easy, yet for Joseph to see his loved father die, rich in faith, must have brought to him great comfort. It must also have given him great consolation, that he had tenderly cared for his father in the sunset of his life and had been with him to the very end of the road. Here is a precious lesson for children to learn, that as parents grow older, it affords opportunity to show the consideration, love and care, which, after all, is only but a duty, in recompense for all the love and care they themselves experienced in early and tender years. In losing his father, Joseph had sustained a great loss. What a joy it had been to him to have had his aged father with him for these past seventeen years! As mentioned earlier, in Joseph's first seventeen years it had been his father's joy to care for him; now in the last seventeen years, it was Joseph's joy to provide and care for his father. No longer was he to hear those words of truth and wisdom from Jacob's mouth which he had so often heard. Those hands which were laid on the heads of Ephraim and Manasseh in blessing, assuring them of divine favors, through being linked with the covenant which God had made with Abraham, Isaac, and Jacob, never again would be raised to perform this sacred act. Like Joseph we sorrow, when we have to part with those who cared for us, guided us, and instructed us. Maybe we did not appreciate their untiring efforts as we ought, but as years wear on, and the day of parting comes, we then see things in a different light. This is also true in relation to men, who from the Holy Scriptures sought to guide and instruct the Christians of their day, for when such men leave us we are made to feel the tremendous loss. Thank God, it is true regarding each one of them, "He, being dead, yet speaketh" (Heb. 11:4). May those who seek to fill the places of these honored servants, emulate them to such an extent, that when their day of service ends, they likewise will be missed.

235

CHAPTER 48

THE BURIAL OF JACOB

Joseph now sets about carrying out the dying wishes of his father concerning his burial. Although Jacob left no instructions as to the manner of it, his whole concern was the place of it. Joseph called in physicians to embalm his body. To be embalmed was a great honor, entailed much expense and was usually reserved for the great. No doubt Joseph had two reasons for doing this: (1) He certainly wanted to bestow great honor on his father—he honored him in life, and now he would honor him in death; (2) Because of the long journey to Canaan, and the time that would elapse before the actual burial would take place, embalming would be necessary. As a true and faithful servant he goes to Pharaoh and begs leave of absence, saying, "Let me go up, I pray thee, and bury my father, and I will come again." And Pharaoh said, "Go and bury thy father, according as he made thee swear."

Genesis 50:7-14 describes for us that outstanding event. Never was there such a funeral procession known to leave the land of Egypt en route for Canaan. "And Joseph went up to bury his father: and with him went up all the servants of Pharaoh, the elders of his house, and all the elders of the land of Egypt, and all the house of Joseph, and his brethren, and his father's house: only their little ones, and their flocks, and their herds, they left in the land of Goshen. And there went up with him both chariots and horsemen: and it was a very great company. And they came to the threshing floor of Atad, which is beyond Jordan, and there they mourned with a great and very sore lamentation: and he made a mourning for his father seven days. And when the inhabitants of the land, the Canaanites, saw the mourning in the floor of Atad, they said, This is a grievous mourning to the Egyptians: wherefore the name of it was called Abel-mizraim, which is beyond Jordan. And his sons did unto him according as he commanded them: for his sons carried him into the land of Canaan, and buried him in the cave of the field of Machpelah, which Abraham bought with the field for a possession of a burying place of Ephron the Hittite, before Mamre. And Joseph returned into Egypt, he, and his brethren, and all that went up with him to bury his father, after he had buried his father."

CHAPTER 49

THE BRETHREN FEAR JOSEPH

Now that their father has been buried, and Joseph is still retaining his high-ranking position in Egypt, Joseph's brethren thought the time had now arrived for Joseph to have his revenge. Their guilty consciences were aroused; they were stung with remorse for their own former conduct, and tormented with the apprehension that the time of retribution was at hand. "And when Joseph's brethren saw that their father was dead, they said, Joseph will peradventure hate us, and will certainly requite us all the evil which we did unto him. And they sent a messenger unto Joseph, saying, Thy father did command before he died, saying, so shall ye say unto Joseph, Forgive, I pray thee now, the trespass of thy brethren, and their sin; for they did unto thee evil: and now, we pray thee, forgive the trespass of the servants of the God of thy father. And Joseph wept when they spake unto him" (Gen. 50:15-17).

Who were the messengers Joseph's brethren sent to solicit his pardon? Would Benjamin be one of them? Perhaps he was, for he had no need of forgiveness. Evidently they were afraid themselves to enter into the presence of Joseph, so great were their fears. How mistaken they were, and how little they really knew of Joseph's heart! Had he not spoken the word of forgiveness seventeen years ago? Had he not placed on each of their cheeks the kiss of reconciliation, and for all these years nourished them and their families as he had promised? Listen to how he bore with these guilt-laden men. In verse 16 the messenger had to begin by saying to Joseph, "Thy father did command before he died, saying, Forgive, I pray thee . . ."

We are caused to ask, Did Jacob really leave orders for this message to be carried to Joseph? There is great reason to think that he did not; he knew Joseph too well to know that such a message was not necessary. If he had, he would have made solicitations to Joseph before he died. The opening words of their request are therefore to be considered as the words of Joseph's own brethren, and not of his father. The liberty which they used was most unwarranted. It was the urge of a guilty conscience to use a lie for strengthening their appeal and to gain the assurance of Joseph's forgiveness. The expression they used, "Forgive, I pray thee, now, the trespass of thy brethren," produced a strong motive for pardon. It was to a brother they were appealing, and when they added, "Forgive the trespass of the servants of the God of thy father" this strengthened the motive for pardon all the more. No wonder Joseph wept when they spake unto him.

It was distressing that they should question his forgiving love and grace, after being for these seventeen years recipients of his tender care and bountiful provision. From the day he made himself known unto them, assuring them of his full and free forgiveness, had they ever seen the slightest change in his attitude toward them? Joseph knew that the petition was not the words of his father, but at the same time he also knew that what they expressed would have been his father's mind in the case which his brethren supposed. The mention, too, of "the God of thy father" supplied them with the strongest of arguments that they should have a favorable hearing. They felt they had a weighty

239

plea when they asked forgiveness for their father's sake, for they knew how close was the bond that existed between Joseph and his father, but when they added they were pleading as the servants of "the God of thy father," this brought the matter into a higher court, as we shall see from Joseph's reply.

How sorely wounded was that heart of love, that they should doubt his spoken word of pardon given so long ago! Joseph, however, knew it was the scourge of a guilty conscience opening up the memories of their past sin, and enforcing the solemn fact that "God requireth that which is past," and that it was impossible to escape divine retribution. Surely his brethren had cried to God for forgiveness, knowing that what they had done was not only sin against Joseph, but sin against God, and if they had done so sincerely and with repentance, then their sin was forgiven. Of course, while it is true that on the ground of full confession God will forgive the act, yet the consequences and fruits remain. This is a divine principle and runs right through the pages of Holy Scripture.

CHAPTER 50

FORGIVENESS ASSURED

What a spectacle of humiliation and confusion is seen in verse 18! Joseph is standing weeping, while they, to a man, are fallen before him with their faces to the earth. They could get no lower, and as they lie they cry, "Behold, we be thy servants" (v. 18). Now for Joseph's reply: "And Joseph said unto them, Fear not: for am I in the place of God?" (v. 19). The first two words were surely most assuring: "Fear not." They certainly had fear—the paralyzing fear of retribution. This was only too evident to Joseph, hence this gracious utterance, "Fear not." It is only tyrants who can delight to see anyone convulsed with fear, and grievously tormented in spirit, but this was not Joseph. It was his earnest desire to banish from the minds of his brethren every gloomy and disquieting thought. When he asks the question, "Am I in the place of God?" he would bear testimony to God's sole authority as the Avenger of sin; he would not presume to take God's place "to whom vengeance belongeth." Joseph lived long before the time when God said through Moses, "To Me belongeth vengeance, and recompense" (Deut. 32:35; see also Rom. 12:19). Yet it is plain to be seen that Joseph knew the truth taught in these important words. What can be more presumptuous than for any man, no matter how exalted his position in this life, to usurp the prerogatives of the Judge of all the earth!

How the attitude of Joseph on this occasion reminds us of our Lord Jesus Christ, as spoken of in 1 Peter 2:23: "Who, when He was reviled, reviled not again; when He suffered, He threatened not; but committed Himself to Him that judgeth righteously." He even made intercession for those transgressors who crucified Him. Here surely is a plain lesson for all who name the name of Christ: when wronged, when evilly entreated, and sorely grieved, they should follow Joseph's example, and the supreme example of the blessed Lord, leave the case in God's hand, whose sole prerogative it is to judge.

Joseph, instead of upbraiding them, or adding to their torment, said, "But as for you, ye thought evil against me: but God meant it unto good, to bring to pass, as it is this day, to save much people alive. Now therefore fear ye not: I will nourish you, and your little ones. And he comforted them, and spake to their hearts" (Gen. 50:20, 21, margin). Had they known Psalm 103:10 they could have joined with the Psalmist and said, "He hath not dealt with us after our sins; nor rewarded us according to our iniquities." This is exactly the God-like way that Joseph dealt with his unworthy brethren. Looking back over his life's history with all its varying circumstances, Joseph could see the outworking of the plan of God. His mention of their evil intentions, was only to throw these into contrast with the gracious intention of the God of his fathers, which included not only the preservation of Jacob and his family, but the saving of "much people alive." This was a reference to the Egyptians whose lives were preserved, because of the God-given wisdom vouchsafed to him in the preparation he made for the devastating years of famine.

Sometimes even the devoted Christian finds it hard to understand the reason for life's checkered pathway, with its many trials and disappointments. For a time the south wind blows softly and the going is good, then suddenly and abruptly the storm breaks and all is changed. Sometimes it is a break-down in health, which seems to blur future prospects; at other times bereavement may rob one of his dearest and most needed loved ones, and as a result he is crushed beneath a burden of sorrow. In this connection I am reminded of the poet's words:

> *Not till the loom is silent,*
> *And the shuttles cease to fly,*
> *Will God unroll the canvas*
> *And explain the reason why*
> *The dark threads were as needful*
> *In the skillful Weaver's hand,*
> *As the threads of gold and silver*
> *In the pattern He has planned.*

The saintly Rutherford of Anworth, looking back over the rugged pathway of life, which for him was beset with many a sore trial, left us these precious and meaningful words:

> *With mercy and with judgment*
> *My web of time He wove,*
> *And aye the dews of sorrow*
> *Were lustered with His love.*
> *I'll bless the hand that guided,*
> *I'll bless the heart that planned,*
> *When throned where glory dwelleth,*
> *In Immanuel's land.*

There was the day when Jacob wailed out, "All these things are against me," yet even on this side of time he learned, that when he thought the wheels were going in the reverse, they were actually going straight for-

243

ward in God's plan for his good and blessing. The tried Christian, who might never find out the reason why while here on earth will in that coming day of glory be made to understand fully and, like Rutherford, will "bless the hand that guided, and bless the heart that planned."

CHAPTER 51

LESSONS FROM THE DIVINE PLAN

Having heard Joseph assuring his brethren of his unchanged attitude toward them, we are nearing the end of our story which, I am sure, the reader will agree is one of the greatest on the pages of human history. What valuable lessons we might learn from it! Here, too, are solemn warnings to avoid envy, jealousy and hatred, the very things which incited the brethren of Joseph to carry out their wicked and evil intentions to get rid of him, and which caused them years of torment and constant fear of divine retribution. Over against this, we see in the life and conduct of Joseph the value of a life lived in the fear of God, and of having His accompanying presence through the shaded as well as the sunlit paths of life. What grace was seen in his daily life from start to finish, whether grinding in the prison or governing the people. Whether in humiliation or exaltation, there were graces which marked him out as a most outstanding type of our Lord Jesus Christ who was "full of grace and truth" (John 1:14). Some of the graces that adorned the life of Joseph are embraced in Philippians 4:8—things that are true, things that are honest, things that are just, things that are pure, things that are lovely, things that are of good report. The Christian might well hear the Spirit's voice, as he looks at Joseph, saying, "Whose faith follow."

Reluctantly, I bring my reader to the last five verses of the great book of Genesis, which book has been well termed "The seed plot of the Bible." Verse 22 says,

"And Joseph dwelt in Egypt, he, and his father's house: and Joseph lived an hundred and ten years." Hebrews 11:9 tells us, "By faith he [Abraham] sojourned in the land of promise, as in a strange country, dwelling in tabernacles with Isaac and Jacob, the heirs with him of the same promise." In this Joseph differed from his progenitors; for approximately seventy years he dwelt in a palace in Egypt, honored by the whole nation, and by the surrounding nations as the wisest and greatest of men. While this is true, yet the faith that marked Abraham, Isaac and Jacob as they dwelt in their moveable tents, was the same faith that marked the illustrious Joseph in his palatial residence. Despite his exalted station in Egypt, he valued the promise of Canaan more than all the honors bestowed on him by Pharaoh and the people of that land; and looked forward with great pleasure to the day when Ephraim and Manasseh would count it the highest honor to be numbered among the tribes of Israel, and share in the inheritance promised to Abraham. Indeed, Joseph himself counted it a much greater honor to be the son of Jacob, than the governor of Egypt.

The fact that Joseph dwelt in Egypt all these years does not mean that this was of his own choosing. He simply arrived there at the beginning by divine leading, and he recognized it was the will of God that he should dwell there and be a father to Pharaoh, and the shepherd of Israel. No doubt his old father also had told him of God's word to him at Beer-sheba, that it was in Egypt God would make him a great nation. Joseph would also be well acquainted with the fact that when God promised to Abraham (in Genesis 15:14) that he would give the land of Canaan to his seed, he also informed him, that he and his seed should be sojourners in a land that was not theirs, for the space of four hundred and fifty years. The one half of that period their abode would be in the land of Canaan, as in a strange land, and the other half would be in the land of Egypt.

Surely the sons of Jacob, now that their father had gone, would appreciate the goodness of God in giving them the benefit of Joseph's protection and care. Little did they know that day at Dothan when it was in their heart to kill him, that they were forming a scheme that would end in their own destruction, if they had done so. Many times they must have blessed the God of their fathers for confounding their evil designs and that his valuable life had been preserved from their own wicked hands, and also that God had raised him to such an exalted position, thus making it possible for him to be their saviour in the years of famine, and to provide for them a home in the rich pastures of Goshen.

Verse 22 gives us the span of Joseph's life, one hundred and ten years. He did not reach the years of his father, and many eminent men who came after him lived longer than he did. But, after all, what does it matter whether life is long or short? The important thing is that the time has been well spent so as to earn divine approval when the day of reckoning arrives. The Lord Jesus Christ, cut off at the age of thirty-three, could say to His Father, "I have glorified Thee on the earth; I have finished the work which Thou gavest Me to do." It is said of John the Baptist, who was about the same age as his Master, and who was decapitated by the wicked Herod, that he "fulfilled his course" (Acts 13:25). Certainly Joseph's life was a full one, and one which brought blessing to thousands; a life which ended without a blot and without a regret. Where is the follower of Christ who would not covet such an ending, let life be long or short?

We are not told here of the happenings in the land of Goshen in the years that intervened from the time of Jacob's death until Joseph's death, but we learn from the first chapter of Exodus of their prolific growth. We read in Exodus 1:5-7, "And all the souls that came out of the loins of Jacob were seventy souls: for Joseph was in Egypt already. And Joseph died, and all his brethren, and all that generation. And the children of Israel were fruitful, and increased abundantly, and multiplied, and waxed exceeding mighty; and the land was filled with them." In this we see the promise made to Jacob at Beer-sheba fulfilled to the letter, "I will there make of thee a great nation."

The last word we get of Joseph in Genesis is that "Joseph saw Ephraim's children of the third generation: the children also of Machir the son of Manasseh were brought up upon Joseph's knees." We do not find that Joseph had any more children by Asenath save his two sons, nor did he marry another wife to increase his family, but was content with Ephraim and Manasseh of his own body, in the prospect of thousands and millions of descendants in the latter days, according to the covenant promise. The Bible speaks of children's children as the glory of old men. Surely this was the portion of the aged Joseph as his eyes were allowed to feast on the third generation before he departed this life. Having admired the noble characteristics of Joseph's life, we have an idea how the sons and their children would be brought up in the faith of their fathers, and made to appreciate the honor of being children of the covenant.

Here parents may learn a valuable lesson. How much depends upon the character of the parents' lives, and the kind of example given! Although Joseph had no Bible, he practiced the truth of Proverbs 22:6, "Train up a child in the way he should go: and when he is old, he will not depart from it." Looking at parent-life from this angle, shows the grave responsibility attached thereto. The lead given to the child is not only going to influence him for this life but help to determine for him the weal or woe of that life to come. This means that if a child is taught to fear God, reverence His Word, and embrace His salvation, the result will be a God-honoring life in this world, and a home in glory in the next. On the other hand, if there be no true guidance given to the child, and no wise instruction for the difficult path of life, and if the necessity for fearing God and of reverencing His Word are neglected, what can be expected but a wayward, useless life, and eternal ruin at the end.

At the beginning of our story it was ours to look at a charming Hebrew lad moving about the home in Shechem wearing the "coat of many colors" as the pride of a father's heart. Through these many pages we have traveled in mind with him through life's checkered pathway. We have seen him loved, hated, sold into slavery, falsely accused, unjustly condemned, grinding in prison, yet through all this "the Lord was with him." Then the tables turned and on account of his God-given wisdom he was lifted from prison and exalted to the governorship of Egypt. Recognized as the saviour of the land, he rescued his father, brethren and families from the ravages of famine in the land of Canaan, planted them in the rich pastures of Goshen, nourished them, rewarded his brethren good for evil, tended his father to the last, and at his request buried him with great honors in the land of Canaan. He then returned to Egypt to his responsible post and to be occupied still with the care of his father's family, such care being attended with the consciousness that he was doing eminent service for the God of his fathers, preparing the way for the great things which had been promised to Abraham, Isaac, Jacob, and their seed. His indeed was a "work of faith and a labour of love."

CHAPTER 52

JOSEPH'S TRIUMPHANT END

All that we are left to consider concerning the great and God-honoring life of Joseph is its glorious and triumphant ending. There is no lamenting, no complaining, no remorse, and no dread of the "pale horse and his rider." Death's cold waters seem to him unruffled and tranquil. His end would remind us of Psalm 37:37, "Mark the perfect man, and behold the upright: for the end of that man is peace." Knowing the death-knell was about to sound we read that Joseph called his brethren, and said unto them, "I die: and God will surely visit you, and bring you out of this land unto the land which he sware to Abraham, to Isaac, and to Jacob" (Gen. 50:24). He was not concerned in the slightest with that strange mysterious moment of his exodus. He is filling the role of the prophet speaking to his brethren of a day that was sure to come, when God would visit them, bring them out of Egypt, and plant them in the land of promise. Joseph was not afraid to die, for he had lived in such a manner, that the symptoms of his approaching dissolution gave him no concern. All his thoughts were for his brethren, and he did what he could to console them, and to comfort them, with the absolute certainty of the promise of the covenant-keeping God. He assured them God would be with them, and their seed after them, bringing them through all the tribulations that would mark their pathway, until the day when they would take their departure from Egypt.

Having said this, we read in verse 25, "And Joseph took an oath of the children of Israel, saying, God will surely visit you, and ye shall carry up my bones from hence." Although he himself was not allowed to quit Egypt for Canaan, he, like his old father Jacob, would take an oath of the children of Israel, that when the exodus from Egypt eventually would come, they would take with them his bones, and bury them in the land of his fathers. He was "strong in faith," resting in the word of his faithful God, who had been his daily companion throughout all the trials and triumphs of life.

When we reach New Testament times, and Calvary's atoning sufferings are completed, and Joseph of Arimathea's new tomb is emptied, the Lord Jesus Christ, who burst the bands of death, has become the "firstfruits of them that slept" (1 Cor. 15:20). Thereby He destroyed him that had the power of death, that is, the devil; and delivered them who through fear of death were all their lifetime subject to bondage (see Heb. 2: 14, 15). By this triumphant act and victory over death, hell and the grave, Christ removed the sting of death for the Christian, making that strange and mysterious moment of departure but a falling asleep, to wake up in the glory of heaven's eternal home, and to see the Saviour face to face. No wonder Paul said to the Philippian church, "For I am in a strait betwixt two, having a desire to depart, and to be with Christ; which is far better: nevertheless to abide in the flesh is more needful for you" (Phil. 1:23, 24). How beautifully Miss Carson expressed it in her lovely hymn:

> *O death! O grave! I do not dread your power,*
> *The ransom's paid;*
> *On Jesus, in that dark and dreadful hour,*
> *My guilt was laid.*

251

And now He's risen; proclaim the joyful story,
The Lord's on high!
And we in Him are raised to endless glory,
And ne'er can die.

Like Joseph, the Lord Jesus Christ, before He died, gathered His own around Him in the upper room, that He might console and comfort them. He knew that their hearts were filled with sorrow, because of His going away. As Joseph told his brethren God would be with them, so the Saviour told His own that He would not leave them orphans. He said, "I will pray the Father, and He shall give you another Comforter, that He may abide with you for ever; even the Spirit of truth; . . . ye know Him; for He dwelleth with you, and shall be in you" (John 14:16, 17).

All down the years, since that session in the upper room, what a comfort the Christian has received from these undying words of John 14:1-3, "Let not your heart be troubled: ye believe in God, believe also in me. In my Father's house are many mansions: if it were not so, I would have told you. I go to prepare a place for you. And if I go and prepare a place for you, *I will come again,* and receive you unto myself; that where I am, there ye may be also." This Paul calls the "blessed hope" (Titus 2:13). Joseph held out the prospect of an earthly land, flowing with milk and honey for the seed of Abraham, but Christ directs the Christian to the mansions of Glory, to be entered at His coming again. Reader, is this your glad hope? If you are resting on the value of His atoning sacrifice accomplished on Calvary, then well may you rejoice. Should this definite and personal trust be lacking in your life up until this present moment, why not do it now? How sad to miss the day of His coming and find oneself on the wrong side of Heaven's door!

CHAPTER 53

JOSEPH IS DEAD

Having reached the last verse in Genesis in the story of our great Joseph we read, "So Joseph died, being an hundred and ten years old: and they embalmed him, and he was put in a coffin in Egypt." All his honor, fame, riches and goodness, could not prevent him from the ruthless hand of the "last enemy." Yet, as we have seen, he faced it without a tremor, for well he knew his death would not be his destruction, but the gateway into the regions of the blest. Like his father, Joseph, instead of being interred in Canaan, could have had a burial in Egypt, with all the publicity and honor attached to his high ranking position, being next to Pharaoh on the throne, and his body laid to rest in a magnificent Egyptian tomb. But this was not for Joseph.

It is true that Joseph had spent only the first seventeen years of his life in Canaan, yet he still looked upon it as his home, even though the last seventy years of his life were spent enjoying great favors from the king and people of Egypt. To make sure then that he would not be left to lie with the princes of Egypt, he took an oath from the children of Israel, to make sure that his last resting place on earth would be in the land, which God sware to Abraham, Isaac, and Jacob. Being so fully persuaded of the truth and the goodness of the covenant promise, by faith he "gave commandment concerning his bones" (Heb. 11:22).

When Sarah died, though Abraham loved her dearly, we find him asking for a place where he might bury her out of his sight, for she could no longer be the desire of his eyes when she became a prey to corruption. In Joseph's case this was unnecessary, as no expense was spared in the embalming of his body by the Egyptian physicians; so skillfully was this done, that a body could be kept indefinitely from going to corruption, and was even pleasant to look upon. When we remember how long it would be before he would be buried in that land of his fathers, we can see the absolute necessity for his body being embalmed.

The very last statement in the book of Genesis stands out in vivid contrast to its majestic first statement, "In the beginning God," for here we end with "a coffin in Egypt." As years advanced, and the throne of Egypt was filled by another king who knew not Joseph, and because the seed of Jacob had grown into a multitude, he said to the people, "Behold, the people of the children of Israel are more and mightier than we: Come on, let us deal wisely with them; lest they multiply, and it come to pass, that, when there falleth out any war, they join also unto our enemies, and fight against us, and so get them up out of the land. Therefore they did set over them taskmasters to afflict them with their burdens. And they built for Pharaoh treasure cities, Pithom and Raamses. But the more they afflicted them, the more they multiplied and grew" (Exod. 1:9-12). Instead now of being honored guests in the land of Egypt, they are reduced to slavery, with its cruel bondage. Even with all this Joseph's dying hopes were not disappointed, for when the day of redemption and deliverance came under Moses, despite the hurry of their departure, and the immense load of business and care which lay upon his mind, he did not forget the bones of Joseph.

254

CHAPTER 54

JOSEPH'S CHARGE HONORED

In Exodus 13:19 we read, "And Moses took the bones of Joseph with him: for he had straitly sworn the children of Israel, saying, God will surely visit you; and ye shall carry up my bones away hence with you." None of the men to whom the oath had been administered were then in the land of the living. But the oath that they had sworn was not dead. Moses would have felt guilty of the basest ingratitude, if not sin against God, had he neglected to carry out the request of the dying patriarch. So then, for forty years during Israel's wilderness wanderings Joseph's coffin was carried, and even though Moses was not allowed to see its last resting place, eventually under the leadership of Joshua, and after all these years of waiting, Shechem was reached.

Yes, the very Shechem where, as a lad, Joseph moved among his brethren wearing the "coat of many colors," the joy of his aged father's heart. That beautiful coat was to become the central point round which the whole history of Joseph revolved. What a contrast it was to the coat which was wrapped about his bones by the physicians of Egypt to prevent the workings of corruption, during the longest recorded funeral in the pages of Holy Scripture. Joshua 24:32 reads, "And the bones of Joseph, which the children of Israel brought up out of Egypt, buried they in Shechem, in a parcel of ground

255

which Jacob bought of the sons of Hamor . . . for an hundred pieces of silver: and it became the inheritance of the children of Joseph." There Joseph's remains lie, until the resurrection morning.

What precious dust has lain all these centuries also in the cave of Machpelah awaiting that great day of resurrection at the coming of our Lord Jesus Christ! While here on earth He told the empty and vain religionists, "Ye shall see Abraham, Isaac and Jacob, and all the prophets, in the kingdom of God, and you yourselves thrust out." I have often tried to picture what a meeting that will be when these great heroes of faith meet in "The Eternal City." Indeed when we think of that morning when the graves of land and sea shall yield up the bodies of all those who have died in faith, when corruption shall put on incorruption, and mortal shall put on immortality (1 Cor. 15:53). "What a gathering of the ransomed that will be!" Is it any wonder Paul by the Spirit told the Thessalonians, who mourned their dead, to look to that day of reuniting, when the dead in Christ would rise, and the living would be caught up together with them, to be forever with the Lord? I repeat, is it any wonder he said to them in light of that day, "Comfort one another with these words" (1 Thess. 4:13-18)? With joy the Christian sings:

> *Jesus is coming! sing the glad word!*
> *Coming for those He redeemed by His blood,*
> *Coming to reign as the glorified Lord!*
> > *Jesus is coming again!*

> *Jesus is coming! The dead shall arise,*
> *Loved ones shall meet in a joyful surprise,*
> *Caught up together to Him in the skies:*
> > *Jesus is coming again!*

As we watch the nation of Israel leave the land of bondage with the body of Joseph, to have it with them every day during those forty years in the wilderness, we are reminded of a very precious truth in the New Testament. They had in their midst until they reached the end of their wilderness journeyings the "memorials of death," but when their destination was reached these were dispensed with. While they carried the bones of Joseph, it would call to mind the greatness of his person and work in the land of Egypt, as the saviour of the land. Every step of the journey would speak out his unwavering faith in the God of his fathers, and the promise given them of inheriting the land. Every time they looked at that coffin it should have given them assurance that the covenant-keeping God would carry out His word without fail, and give them a national home, which they could call their very own.

Turning to the New Testament, we shall gather in thought with Christ and His disciples in the Upper Room, where they kept the Passover. It was the night of His betrayal, and Gethsemane and Calvary were just ahead. He was going to leave His disciples in this world as His witnesses, soon they were to see Him ascend from Olivet's mountain. Knowing their sorrow of heart, and the loneliness these disciples were bound to feel when He would leave them, and also the long waiting period that lay ahead of the Church ere He would return, He instituted the "Feast of Memorial" called by Paul "The Lord's Supper." In 1 Corinthians 11:23 we read that this is what the Lord did after they had partaken of the Passover Supper, for according to John 13:26, 30, when Judas had received the sop at the Passover Supper, "He went immediately out and it was night." It was after the betrayer had gone, and He was left with only His own true and loyal disciples, that He introduced this Divine ordinance.

257

As in the case of Israel, who had with them the "Memorials of Death" while they carried the bones of Joseph every step of the journey, until the wilderness with its trials and difficulties was ended, so the Saviour was now going to leave with His own the "Memorials" of His death for the Church's sojourn on earth, until the last step of the journey would be taken and Heaven reached. It was His desire, that these emblems during the time of His absence would, in a most telling way, call Him to mind, for how true is the oft-repeated saying, "Out of sight out of mind." Space and time do not allow me to deal in detail with the record given of the Lord's Supper in Matthew, Mark and Luke, much as I would like, because each account has its own significant points of interest. I pass on to 1 Corinthians 11:23, where Paul records for the Church the special revelation given to him by the ascended Lord. As you read the passage, I would ask you to consider seven prominent ideas contained therein.

1. *It is an* ORDINANCE. Verse 23 reads, "For I have received of the Lord that which also I delivered unto you, That the Lord Jesus the same night in which He was betrayed took bread." It is an ordinance, because it was given by the Lord to Paul to be observed by the Church. It is not an ordinance of man; it is a Divine ordinance.

2. *It is* SYMBOLIC. The symbols used were bread and wine. Verses 23 and 24 record "He took bread: and when He had *given thanks,* He brake it, and said, Take, eat: this is My body, which is broken for you: this do in remembrance of Me." The bread was the symbol of His body, and that bread broken is a symbol of Calvary's death. Verse 25 reads, "After the same manner also He took the cup, when He had supped [that is, after the Passover Supper, from which Judas went

out], saying, This cup is the new testament in My blood: this do ye, as oft as ye drink it, in remembrance of Me." The cup containing the wine was the symbol of His blood, to be poured out at Calvary.

3. *It is a* THANKSGIVING. Before dispensing the bread, and giving them the cup to drink, He *gave thanks.* By so doing He was showing this must always be the procedure when partaking of the Supper; although only one audibly does so, he is voicing the thanks of the assembled church.

4. *It is a* MEMORIAL. Verses 24-25 also include this thought, for after He had given thanks for both the bread and the cup, He added, "This do in remembrance of Me." He intended it to be a Memorial Supper, the observance of which would call Him to mind. If Israel had in Joseph's bones, the "memorials of death," the Church today has these sacred emblems in the midst of the gathered company, memorials of His body broken and His blood shed on dark Calvary. How often I have sung with the assembled ·company:

> *Sweet the feast of love divine!*
> *Broken bread and outpoured wine;*
> *Sweet memorials, till the Lord*
> *Call us round His heavenly board,*
> *Some from earth, from glory some,*
> *Severed only "Till He come."*

Well might we call them "sweet memorials"! If Israel on their wilderness journey would be made to remember the great and noble Joseph as they looked at that oblong box containing his bones, how infinitely higher we rise as we partake of these divinely given emblems, for we call Him to mind who left the radiant glory, and descended to the fathomless depths of Calvary, "All for our sakes, our peace to make." He is the One

259

who by His triumphant resurrection has delivered us from the fear of death, and now sits at His Father's right hand, "living in the power of an indissoluble life," our Saviour right to the end of the road, and with these memorials before us, our minds are drawn to look for His promised coming again.

5. *It is a* COVENANT (or a testament). He said, "This cup is the new testament in My blood" (v. 25). If for Israel Joseph's coffin would call to mind God's unconditional covenant made with Abraham, giving them the right to Canaan, we again go infinitely higher in our remembrance of the Lord, when we grasp the meaning of these words in the partaking of the cup, "This cup is the *new covenant in My blood.*" Luke adds, "shed for you." By that blood the Christian has been redeemed, cleansed, forgiven, justified, sanctified, and glorified. To all who trust in the blood of the new covenant, the message is, "Their sins and iniquities will I remember no more" (Heb. 10:17).

It is the plan of God for the believing remnant of Israel in a day that is yet to come, when in deep repentance they will own Him as their once crucified, but then glorified Messiah, that they will enter into the good of the same new covenant. Hebrews 8:8-13 makes this clear, "Behold, the days come, saith the Lord, when I will make a new covenant with the house of Israel and with the house of Judah: not according to the covenant that I made with their fathers in the day when I took them by the hand to lead them out of the land of Egypt; because they continued not in My covenant, and I regarded them not, saith the Lord. For this is the covenant that I will make with the house of Israel after those days, saith the Lord; I will put My laws into their mind, and write them in their hearts: and I will be to them a God, and they shall be to Me a people: and they shall not teach every man his neighbour, and every man his brother, saying, Know the Lord: for all shall know Me, from the least to the greatest. For I will be merciful to their unrighteousness, and their sins and their iniquities will I remember no more. In that He saith, a new covenant, He hath made the first old [Sinai covenant]. Now that which decayeth and waxeth old is ready to vanish away."

The covenant blessings of the knowledge of God, and the knowledge of sins forgiven so completely that they shall be remembered no more, are to be the portion of saved Israel in that day. But these are the very blessings that are enjoyed by the Church now, and again, while a saved Israel will know the joy of millennial bliss and eternal residence on the New Earth, the Church is destined to an eternal residence with Christ, in the celestial glory of the New Heaven.

6. *It is a* MESSAGE. "Ye do show the Lord's death" (v. 26). The word "show," means "to proclaim as an herald," or "preach." That implies that when the church is gathered together around the emblems, and each individual partakes of the same, the company as a whole is preaching the Lord's death. As the angels look on (as they do; see 1 Cor. 11:10) they witness sinners saved by grace, and cleansed by the blood of Christ, demonstrating the great fact, that all that they are, and have, and ever hope to be, they owe to the Lord's death. The next idea related to the Supper is stated at the end of verse 26, in three words of great significance to the church.

7. *It is a* PLEDGE. "Till He come." In partaking of the Lord's Supper, the Christian not only takes a loving look back to Calvary, but a longing look forward to His coming again. The very emblems carry this "blessed

261

hope." Surely the words often sung by the gathered assemblies are most appropriate:

Lord, we know how true Thy promise
To be with us where we meet;
When in Thy loved Name we gather
To enjoy communion sweet.
Dearer still that looked-for promise
To each waiting, yearning heart,
That we soon shall be with Thee, Lord,
And forever where Thou art.

CHAPTER 55

THE RESTING PLACE

When we arrive at Joshua 24:32, many years have passed since the dying Joseph made his brethren sware that his body would be buried in no other place but the place of his boyhood in the land of Canaan, the land of the covenant-promise. Now the place is reached, his beloved Shechem, and one can almost see with what reverence, and deep feeling the "memorials of death" were deposited in the grave, forever out of sight. Thus we bid farewell to Joseph whom we have traced through his life. We have seen him at the age of six, sheltered and protected on that day when Jacob went out to meet Esau, and then at seventeen when he wore his "coat of many colors." We have observed how he was loved by his father, and envied by his brethren; we have traced him right on through the trials and triumphs of his life, until at last we visualize the burial of his bones at Shechem. I am compelled to admit I can think of no greater on the page of Holy Scripture save our blessed Lord Jesus Christ. True, John the Baptist had a high place given him by the Lord, but I am thinking more of the Old Testament worthies, men who lived and died in faith. In the gallery of "Faith's Heroes," in Hebrews 11, the Holy Spirit's brief comment on the death of Joseph is, "By faith Joseph, when he died, made mention of the departing of the children of Israel; and gave commandment concerning his bones" (v. 22).

The question of Ezekiel 37:3 might be asked with regard to Joseph's bones, "Can these bones live?" Or is Shechem the end of all? The answer to these two questions are given us in Paul's great treatise on the resurrection of those who "die in faith." There we read that at the coming of the Lord Jesus Christ, "this corruptible shall have put on incorruption" (1 Cor. 15: 54). To the Thessalonians the apostle says, "The dead in Christ shall rise first" (1 Thess. 4:16). So we turn away from the tomb, where nothing remains but the dust of the once illustrious Joseph, and look forward with bright anticipation to that great resurrection morning when at the blast of the trumpet, Shechem's tomb will yield up its dead, and Joseph, with all those who have died in faith, "shall be raised incorruptible" to cry in triumph, "O grave, where is thy victory?" (1 Cor. 15:55).

> *The Lord Himself shall come,*
> *And shout the quickening word;*
> *Thousands shall answer from the tomb,*
> *"For ever with the Lord"!*
> *That resurrection word,*
> *That shout of victory—*
> *Resound: "For ever with the Lord"!*
> *Amen, so let it be!*

CONCLUSION

Having reached the end of our story, with so many lessons that all of us might profitably learn, whether young, in the prime of life, or in advanced years, I can only pray, that God will enable us to avoid envy and jealousy such as characterized Joseph's brethren, and never act deceitfully, or cover up sin, as they sought to do, with the consequent plunging of their old father into unutterable grief during those long years of Joseph's absence. May we rather be helped of God to emulate those Christ-like graces manifest in the life and conduct of Joseph. He lived his life in the fear of God, not slavish fear, but reverential fear; when tempted to turn from the path of moral rectitude, his cry was, "How then can I do this great wickedness and sin against God?" Such conduct, in all the varied circumstances of life was so marked, that we read again and again, "And the Lord was with him." Living in the fear of the Lord, he daily enjoyed His presence.

We think of Joseph's patient endurance through the years of sore trial; how true of him are the words spoken of our Lord Jesus Christ by Peter, "When He was reviled, reviled not again; when He suffered, He threatened not" (1 Peter 2:23). How Christ-like Joseph was in all this! When the day came that he could have had his revenge on his brethren, it was far from his thoughts; instead, as soon as he cast his eyes on them, after all his years of suffering, he set on foot the plan to save them, with all they had, from the ravages of the coming famine. For cruelty he returned kindness; for evil he returned good. He honored his father Jacob, cared for him and tended him until his dying hour. He secured by a favor from Pharaoh the rich pastures of Goshen as a home for his brethren and their families. He never changed his attitude or bore any hard feelings against his brethren, and never made any reference to their cruel treatment of him when they rejected him and cast him out.

You will remember his words to the butler in prison, "I was stolen away out of the land of the Hebrews." It could be truly said of him that "the love of God was shed abroad in his heart" (Rom. 5:5). Because he lived daily in the conscious enjoyment of the presence of the Lord, there was produced in him the fruit of the Spirit as outlined in Galatians 5:22, 23: ". . . love, joy, peace, longsuffering, gentleness, goodness, faith, meekness, temperance [self-control]." How clearly he bore the features of Christ, the Heavenly Joseph, of whom Peter says, "He has left us an example that we should follow His steps" (1 Peter 2:21).

To those who read these pages, I must say it is with great reluctance I lay down my pen, and say farewell to "The Coat of Many Colors." I pray that the lessons learned from him who wore it, will live with the Christian and produce a godliness of life and character that shall merit the Lord's approval in that great day of review, when we stand before His judgment seat. What could be more desired in that day, than to hear from His own lips, "Well done, thou good and faithful servant"?

Perchance, you have not yet been linked to the Heavenly Joseph, the once rejected but now glorified Christ. My earnest prayer is that such a link may be formed by your acceptance of the crucified Saviour as your Surety and Substitute. This will give you a guaranteed assurance of a home in Heaven when the journey of life has ended.

Oh, what can equal joy divine?
And what can sweeter be
Than knowing that the soul is safe
For all eternity?
Safe in the Lord without a doubt,
By virtue of the blood,
For nothing can destroy the life
That's hid with Christ in God.

SCRIPTURE INDEX

269

Printed in the United Kingdom
by Lightning Source UK Ltd.
136158UK00001B/1-18/A